Our TEAM

Joan Crawford: From Rags to Riches is a compelling narrative crafted by the ChatStick Team, dedicated to unraveling the complex tapestry of one of Hollywood's most celebrated stars. This book peels back the layers of Joan Crawford's life, from her humble beginnings through the trials and triumphs that led her to become an icon of the silver screen. It is not just a story of fame and success but a testament to resilience, talent, and the indomitable spirit of a woman who refused to be defined by her circumstances. Through meticulous research and heartfelt storytelling, the ChatStick Team invites readers on a journey through the golden age of cinema, guided by the life of a woman who became a legend in her own right.

In this book, readers will find an intricate blend of history, drama, and inspiration. "Joan Crawford: From Rags to Riches" goes beyond the glitz and glamour to reveal the real woman behind the public persona. It offers an intimate look at Crawford's early struggles, her meteoric rise in Hollywood, her most memorable roles, and her lasting influence on the industry and beyond. Crafted with care and admiration for its subject, this book is a tribute to Joan Crawford's enduring legacy and a must-read for anyone fascinated by the stories of those who have shaped our cultural landscape.

chatvariety.com

table of contents

00
Introduction

01
Humble Beginnings

02
The Ascent Begins

03
Breakthrough and Rise to Fame

04
Icon of the Silver Screen

chatvariety.com

table of contents

05
The Woman Behind the Legend

06
Challenges and Resilience

07
Legacy and Influence

08
Conclusion: A Legacy of Transformation and Triumph

chatvariety.com

INTRODUCTION

chapter 01

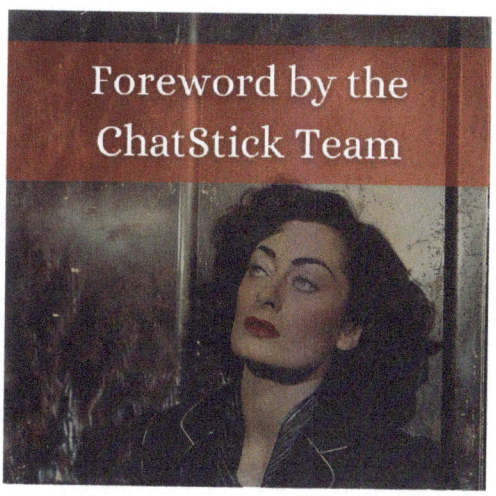

Foreword by the ChatStick Team

Joan Crawford's early years were marked by trials and tribulations that would shape her into the strong, resilient woman she would become. Born on March 23, 1904, as Lucille Fay LeSueur in San Antonio, Texas, Joan grew up in a modest household. Her father, Thomas LeSueur, was a failed opera singer, and her mother, Anna Belle Johnson, worked as a factory laborer. The marriage was tumultuous, marred by frequent arguments and instability.

Tragically, when Joan was still a young child, her father abandoned the family. Left to gather the pieces, Joan's mother relocated to Kansas City, Missouri, in search of better opportunities. It was there that Joan's mother eventually found work as a hotel maid. However, financial struggles persisted, leading Joan to quit school at the age of 12 to help support her family.

Determined to improve their circumstances, Joan's mother enrolled her in dance and theater classes. It was during this time that Joan discovered her passion for performing. She would spend hours honing her dancing skills and practicing monologues, dreaming of a life in the spotlight. Joan's talent and drive caught the attention of her instructors, who recognized her potential and encouraged her to pursue a career in acting.

Joan embraced the opportunities that came her way with fervor. She auditioned for various roles in dance troupes and amateur theaters, often facing rejection but never losing hope. Her perseverance paid off when, at just 16 years old, Joan set her sights on the bright lights and opportunities offered by the bustling city of Chicago. Eager to pursue her dreams, she joined a traveling dance troupe and embarked on a whirlwind adventure across the country.

However, the glamorous life she envisioned was far from reality. The troupe faced financial hardships and often performed in less-than-ideal conditions, testing Joan's resolve at every turn. But she persisted, nurturing her talent and gaining invaluable experience along the way.

In a stroke of fate, Joan's determination caught the attention of a Broadway producer who happened to be in the audience during one of their performances. Impressed by Joan's magnetic stage presence, he offered her a small role in a chorus line. This marked a turning point in her career, as the role opened doors to other opportunities in the burgeoning New York theater scene. Joan's talent and tenacity soon caught the eye of Hollywood scouts seeking fresh faces for the silver screen.

In 1925, Joan Crawford arrived in Hollywood, signing a contract with renowned filmmaker MGM. The studio recognized her potential and was eager to mold her into an iconic star. Under their tutelage, Joan honed her skills and transformed herself into an alluring and sophisticated actress. As the Roaring Twenties unfolded, bringing with it a wave of social change and new freedoms for women, Joan epitomized the modern woman. With her dazzling beauty, undeniable talent, and a determination that burned like a furnace, she swiftly became a rising star in Tinseltown.

In 1928, Joan Crawford made the transition from silent films to talkies, securing her place as a versatile actress capable of adapting to the shifting demands of the film industry. Her dynamic voice and captivating presence on screen captivated audiences across the country. The following year, her performance in "Our Dancing Daughters" solidified her status as a box office draw and propelled her into the realm of stardom.

Throughout the 1930s, Joan Crawford became known for her portrayal of strong and independent women, characters that mirrored her own fierce spirit. From the adventurous socialite in "Grand Hotel" to the resilient working-class woman in "Possessed," Joan's performances captivated audiences and secured her a multitude of prestigious roles. She fearlessly embraced a wide variety of genres, effortlessly transitioning from drama to comedy and even taking on musicals with grace and charm.

Her talent, coupled with a tireless work ethic, garnered Joan critical acclaim and four Academy Award nominations. In 1946, she finally clinched the coveted Oscar for Best Actress for her riveting performance in "Mildred Pierce." The win solidified her status as one of Hollywood's most respected actresses, and she continued to deliver remarkable performances throughout the following decades.

Joan Crawford's personal life was often tumultuous, marked by a series of failed marriages and turbulent relationships. She married four times, each union ending in divorce. Her marriage to actor Franchot Tone was highly publicized and particularly tempestuous. Despite the hardships she faced in her personal life, Joan never allowed it to overshadow her professional achievements.

Even in her later years, Joan Crawford continued to reinvent herself, embracing new mediums such as television and adapting to the changing landscape of entertainment. She starred in her own television series, "The Joan Crawford Show," delighting fans with her magnetic presence once again. Her indomitable spirit and relentless drive served as an inspiration to younger generations of actors who admired her longevity and resilience.

Joan Crawford left an indelible mark on Hollywood and film history. Her influence extends beyond her on-screen performances, as she became an embodiment of the tenacity and determination required to succeed in the often cutthroat entertainment industry. Her legacy continues to inspire aspiring actors and actresses to chase their dreams and overcome the challenges that come their way.

In the following chapters, we will delve deeper into the highs and lows of Joan Crawford's career, her philanthropic endeavors, and the enduring impact she had on the world of cinema. Join us as we unveil the multifaceted woman behind the legend and explore the lasting legacy she left upon the entertainment industry and the hearts of her fans.

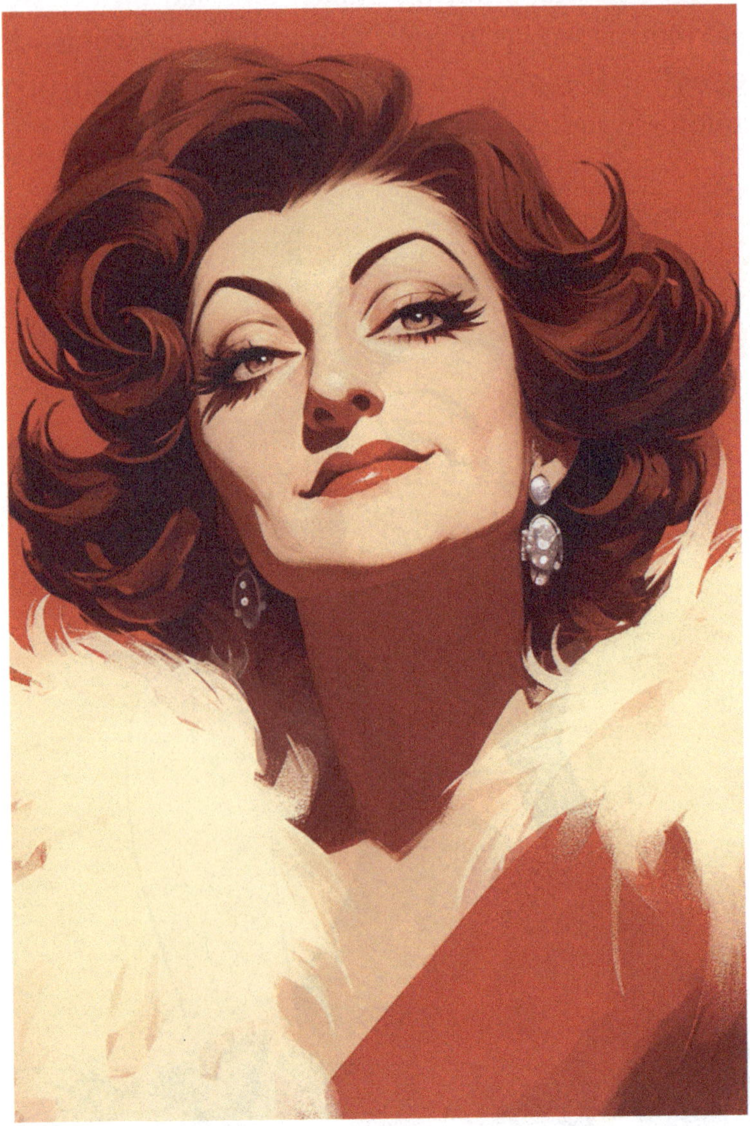

chapter 02

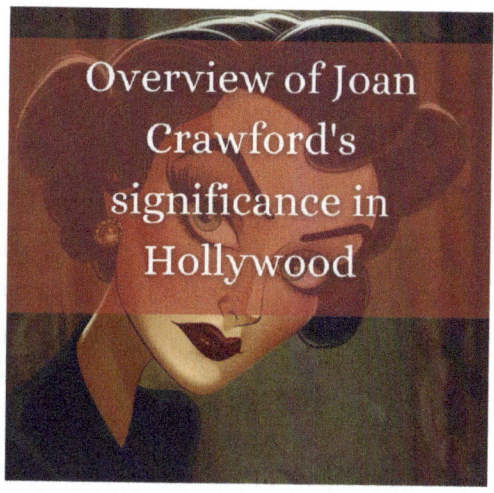

Overview of Joan Crawford's significance in Hollywood

Joan Crawford remains an immortal and captivating figure in the annals of Hollywood. Her presence and impact on the industry are irrefutable, stemming from her multifaceted contributions both in the limelight and behind the scenes. From her groundbreaking roles in the 1920s to her reinvention in the 1940s, Crawford enthralled audiences with her unparalleled talent, compelling beauty, and unwavering determination.

Born Lucille Fay LeSueur in San Antonio, Texas in 1904, Crawford's journey to stardom commenced when she signed with MGM in 1925. This pivotal moment propelled her towards developing her one-of-a-kind style and persona, transforming herself into the quintessential Hollywood star. With her iconic arched eyebrows, radiant complexion, and meticulously sculpted figure, Crawford became the ultimate symbol of beauty and sophistication, inspiring countless women worldwide to emulate her distinctive looks.

Throughout her illustrious career, Crawford embraced a multitude of genres and tackled an array of complex characters, showcasing an extraordinary range as an actress. Her versatility and willingness to take on unconventional roles set her apart, defying societal norms and expectations. During the daring era of pre-Code Hollywood, she fearlessly portrayed strong, independent women who refused to conform to traditional gender roles. By embodying characters with ambition, resilience, and agency, Crawford resonated deeply with audiences, particularly women who saw in her a reflection of their desires for empowerment and autonomy.

One of Crawford's most etched-in-stone performances arrived in the form of the 1945 film "Mildred Pierce," masterfully directed by Michael Curtiz. In this transformative role, Crawford transcended her usual glamorous image to portray a hardworking, compassionate woman who pivots into a successful businesswoman to provide for her family. The film garnered overwhelming critical acclaim and achieved tremendous commercial success, earning Crawford her solitary Academy Award for Best Actress. "Mildred Pierce" marked a pivotal turning point in her career, as it showcased her extraordinary ability to delve into roles with nuanced layers that surpassed the surface-level glamour for which she was renowned.

The significance of Joan Crawford extends beyond her on-screen achievements. She played a defining role in shaping the Hollywood star system and the studio era itself. Driven by ambition and tenacity, Crawford skillfully negotiated her contracts and demanded creative control over her projects. In an era when actors were often at the mercy of studio executives, Crawford meticulously crafted her image and trajectory, empowering herself in an unparalleled manner. Such agency was exceptionally rare for female performers at the time, and Crawford's assertiveness paved the way for future actresses to assert their own influence and autonomy within their careers.

Her mesmerizing image as a paragon of glamour and sophistication was cultivated in collaboration with renowned costume designers, photographers, and hairstylists. Crawford's fashion sense and iconic looks not only influenced trends within the entertainment industry but also captivated the imagination of millions. Whether she graced the red carpet in stunning gowns or effortlessly set trends with her stylish everyday wear, Crawford's sense of style, elegance, and refinement became synonymous with the Hollywood ideal. She became a fashion icon, setting the bar for millions of women around the world who aspired to emulate her poised sophistication and timeless allure.

Beyond her professional achievements, Crawford's personal life also commanded significant attention, further solidifying her status as one of Hollywood's most intriguing and enigmatic personalities. Her marriages, divorces, and high-profile relationships were often splashed across tabloid headlines, providing an ongoing source of fascination for fans and critics alike. Despite personal setbacks and challenges, including her tumultuous relationship with fellow actor and ex-husband, Franchot Tone, Crawford persevered, continuously navigating her private and public life with grace, tenacity, and an unwavering commitment to her craft.

Joan Crawford's impact on Hollywood is an indelible mark that resonates through generations. Her contributions to the industry, both in front of and behind the camera, laid the groundwork for future actors and filmmakers, forever transforming the landscape of cinema. Her enduring legacy serves as a reminder of the immeasurable power of determination, talent, and the unwavering commitment to reinvention.

As we delve further into Joan Crawford's extraordinary life and career in the chapters to come, we will explore the myriad challenges she faced, the tremendous triumphs she achieved, and the lasting impact she left on the world of film. Through her resilient spirit, captivating beauty, and exceptional talent, Crawford solidified her place as an iconic and beloved figure in the annals of Hollywood history, forever engraved in the hearts and minds of movie enthusiasts across the globe.

chatvariety.com

HUMBLE BEGINNINGS

chapter 03

Early life and family background

Joan Crawford, born Lucille Fay LeSueur on March 23, 1905, in San Antonio, Texas, had a humble and challenging background before rising to stardom in Hollywood. Her parents, Thomas E. LeSueur and Anna Bell Johnson, were both theater performers, although their careers were marked by instability and struggle.

Growing up, Crawford often found herself moving from city to city as her parents pursued acting opportunities. Her father, Thomas, a charismatic but troubled man, struggled with alcoholism, leaving the family's life marred by unpredictability and financial strain. His frequent absences and moments of abandonment forced Crawford to learn resilience and self-reliance from an early age.

Despite the hardships, Crawford's mother, Anna Bell, played a vital role in nurturing her daughter's dreams. Anna Bell recognized Lucille's natural talent and encouraged her to express herself creatively. In their modest home, the young girl found solace in the magic of storytelling, constantly immersing herself in books, as literature became both an escape and an inspiration.

Anna Bell's unwavering support brought warmth and stability to Crawford's life, even during their most challenging times. She often took her daughter to see live performances, exposing her to the world of theater and fostering a deep love for the arts. These experiences formed the foundation of Crawford's passion for entertainment and fueled her determination to make her mark in show business.

As her parents' marriage grew increasingly strained, Crawford's father left the family when she was just a teenager. Left with the weight of financial responsibilities, Anna Bell fought to keep her family together. Despite the difficulties, she managed to find stability in Kansas City, Missouri, where they settled and created a home for themselves.

Crawford attended Rockingham Academy, an all-girls boarding school, thanks to her mother's sacrifices and unwavering commitment to her daughter's education. The academy not only provided Lucille with a formal education, but it also nurtured her talent, as she participated in school plays and local theater productions. These early performances captivated her, further fueling her aspirations to pursue a career in acting.

Determined to alleviate her family's financial burden, Crawford took on various part-time jobs while still attending school. She found employment as a model and danced in chorus lines, honing her stage presence and learning the value of hard work. Her relentless spirit and drive propelled her towards the opportunities she needed to break into the world of entertainment.

Tragedy struck once again when Crawford's mother remarried and then divorced, leaving Lucille to face even more instability. Despite these setbacks, she remained resolute in her pursuit of acting. At the age of 17, filled with sheer determination and an unyielding desire for a better life, Crawford made a pivotal decision—she dropped out of school and headed for Chicago, the city that held the promise of a future in the world of show business.

Chicago presented its own set of challenges for Crawford as she navigated the competitive landscape of the entertainment industry. Resourceful and undeterred, she sought out acting classes to refine her skills, investing her time and energy into every opportunity that could bring her closer to her dreams. During this time, she adopted the stage name "Joan Crawford," a moniker she believed possessed a certain allure and potential for success.

Joan Crawford's early life was marked by struggle, uncertainty, and personal hardships, but these very experiences shaped her into the strong, determined woman who would leave an indelible mark in the world of Hollywood. Fueled by her past, she emerged as a force to be reckoned with, her journey from a young, struggling woman to a Hollywood legend just beginning.

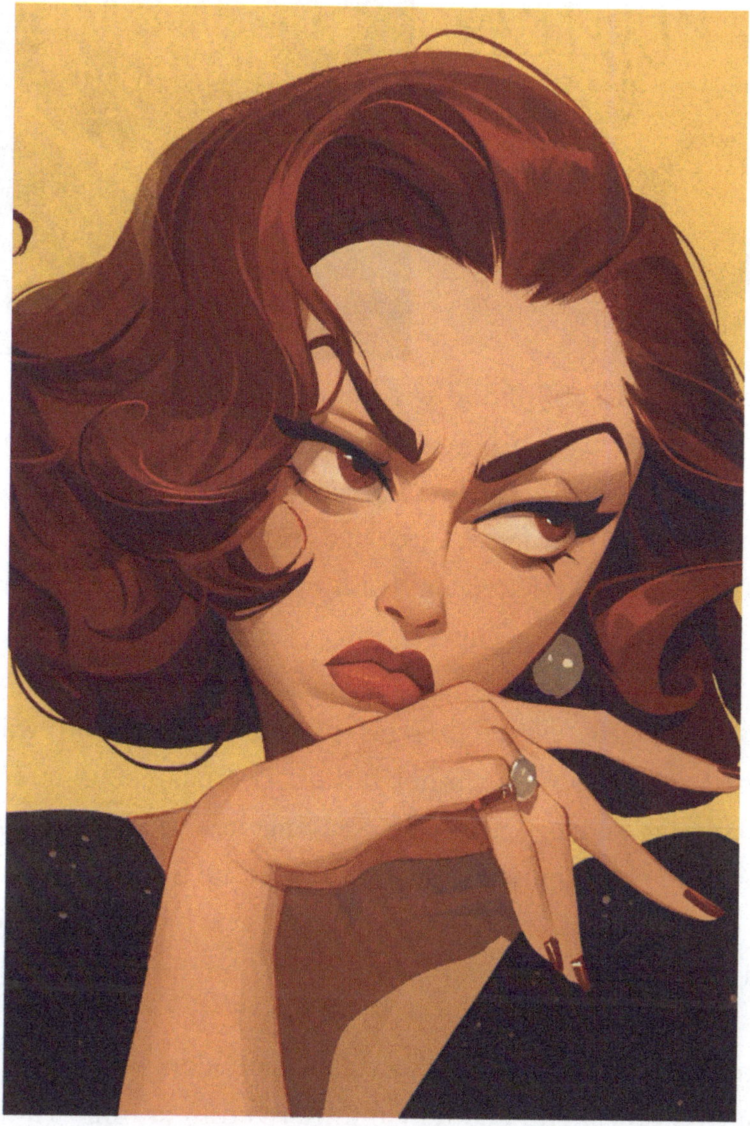

chapter 04

Struggles and hardships of her childhood

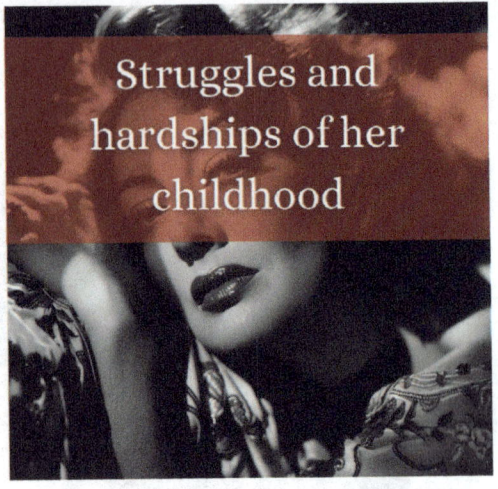

Joan Crawford's childhood was marked by numerous struggles and hardships, which played a significant role in shaping her resilient character and determination to succeed. Born Lucille Fay LeSueur on March 23, 1905, in San Antonio, Texas, she grew up in a poverty-stricken environment that forced her to face adversity from an early age.

One of the greatest challenges of Joan's childhood was her strained relationship with her father, Thomas LeSueur. He was an alcoholic and often absent, leaving her mother, Anna Bell Johnson, to raise Joan and her siblings alone. The instability and emotional turmoil caused by her father's behavior added an extra layer of difficulty to an already challenging situation.

Financial struggles were also a constant companion in Joan's formative years. The LeSueur family lived in cramped and run-down accommodations, frequently moving from one place to another in search of affordable housing. This constant instability led to a lack of permanence and security in Joan's young life, leaving her with a sense of constant uncertainty.

To make ends meet, Joan's mother took on various menial jobs, including sewing, housekeeping, and waiting tables. Joan often accompanied her mother to these jobs, witnessing firsthand the grueling physical labor and long hours her mother endured to provide for the family. These experiences instilled in Joan a strong work ethic and an understanding of the sacrifices one must make to survive.

However, Joan's efforts to help her family were not limited to accompanying her mother to work. At a young age, she also began taking on odd jobs, such as babysitting and selling newspapers, to contribute to the family's income. These early experiences taught her the value of hard work and perseverance and laid the foundation for her future success.

Education was another area where Joan faced obstacles. Due to the family's financial constraints, she had limited access to formal schooling. Instead, Joan sought solace in books, devouring literature whenever she could. She often visited the local library, immersing herself in the worlds created by authors and finding solace and inspiration in their words.

Joan's love for literature became an integral part of her life, fueling her imagination and providing an escape from the harsh realities of her childhood. She cherished her time spent reading, finding solace and inspiration in the stories and characters that captured her heart. This passion for storytelling would later manifest in her career as an actress.

Despite the limitations imposed on her, Joan possessed an innate curiosity and thirst for knowledge. She was an avid learner, utilizing any opportunity to expand her understanding of the world around her. She devoured everything from classic literature to newspapers, eager to absorb as much information as possible and nourish her intellectual growth.

Nevertheless, Joan's childhood was not without its tragedies. Alongside the financial hardships and strained family dynamics, her early years were overshadowed by the tragic loss of her beloved brother, Hal, who died at the age of four from accidental scalding. This loss had a profound impact on Joan and her family, deepening the emotional strain they already endured.

The devastating loss of Hal shattered the family's already fragile stability. Joan's mother, Anna Bell, struggled to cope with the immense grief, and the emotional toll cast a dark shadow over their lives. This profound experience of loss taught Joan the fragility of life and the importance of treasuring every precious moment.

The struggles and hardships of Joan's childhood may have been seemingly insurmountable, but her enduring spirit and determination to escape her circumstances fueled her aspirations to pursue a better life. Her remarkable resilience and unwavering determination to overcome adversity ultimately paved the way for her remarkable rise to fame in the world of entertainment.

Chapter 4 delves into the profound struggles Joan Crawford faced throughout her childhood, shedding light on the circumstances that tested her resilience and formed the foundation for her future success. Understanding the difficulties she overcame allows us to better appreciate the strength and determination that defined her journey from humble origins to Hollywood stardom.

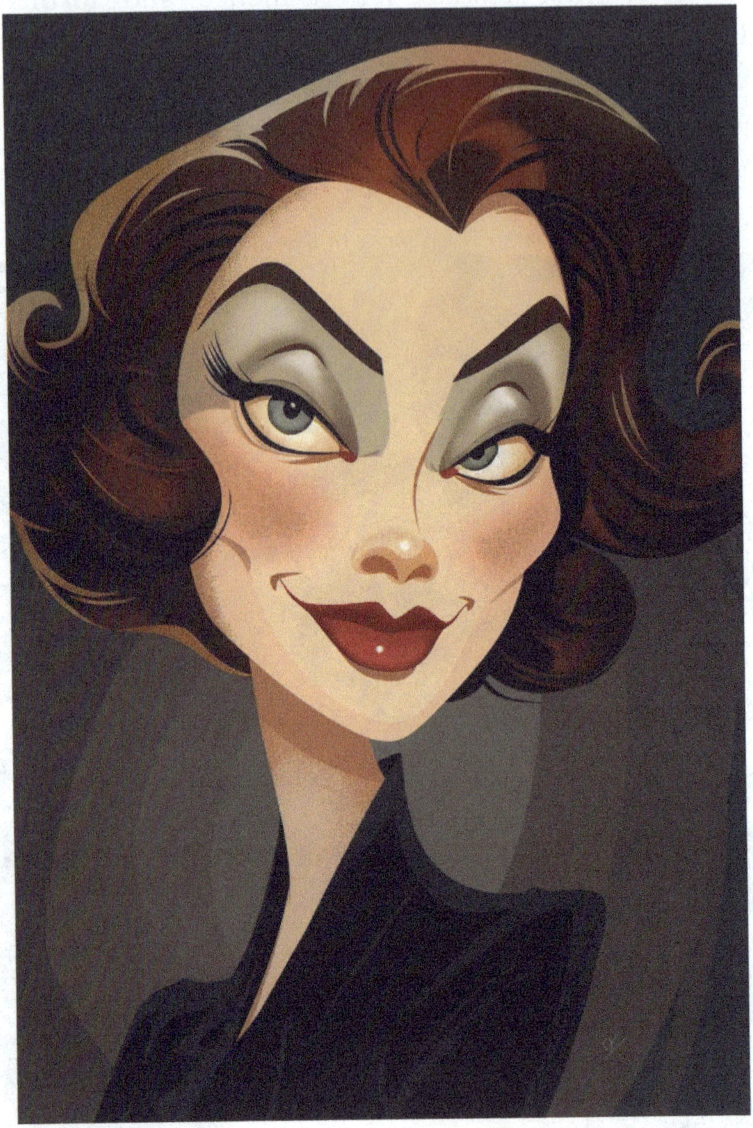

chapter 05

First steps towards acting

Joan Crawford's journey towards becoming an actress was not a smooth one. Born Lucille Fay LeSueur on March 23, 1904, in San Antonio, Texas, she faced numerous struggles and hardships throughout her childhood that would shape her determination and resilience.

Growing up in poverty, Joan's family faced constant financial instability. Her parents, Thomas LeSueur and Anna Bell Johnson, had a tumultuous relationship, and their separation when Joan was young added to the challenges they endured. Despite the difficulties, Lucille had a spark of ambition and a dream of escaping her circumstances.

At the age of 16, Joan enrolled in Stephens College, Columbia, Missouri, where she studied acting and dance. It was here that she discovered her passion for the performing arts. In the college's drama department, she found solace and a platform to express her creativity. With her natural talent and unwavering drive, Joan excelled in her studies and developed a deep appreciation for the craft of acting.

After completing her education, Joan moved to Chicago, eager to pursue her dreams and experience the vibrant theater scene. She immersed herself in the city's artistic community, attending plays and frequenting the local cafes where aspiring actors gathered. She took on any opportunity that came her way, from small roles to helping backstage. Joan's determination and work ethic were unmatched. She tirelessly rehearsed, studied classic plays, and sought guidance from seasoned performers. It was during this time that she honed her skills and learned the intricacies of live performance.

In 1925, Joan made the bold decision to try her luck in Hollywood, the epicenter of the film industry, where dreams were made or shattered. She packed her belongings, including her determination and talent, and embarked on a journey towards her ultimate goal - becoming a successful actress.

Hollywood, however, proved to be a different world altogether. Joan faced countless rejections and setbacks, each one testing her resilience. The competition was fierce, and aspiring actors lined the streets, hoping for their big break. But Joan refused to give up. She knew she had something special to offer, and she would stop at nothing to prove it.

Living off meager savings, Joan persevered with auditions and casting calls. She attended numerous casting agents' offices, hoping to catch a break. But securing a significant role seemed elusive. Often, the roles offered to her were minor, and she found herself in bit parts, barely noticeable on screen. However, Joan embraced every opportunity with grace and dedication. She realized that even in these small roles, she had the chance to showcase her talent and leave a lasting impression. Her commitment to even the tiniest part was unparalleled, as she poured her heart into each performance, no matter how brief.

It was during this period that Joan realized the importance of image and branding in the world of show business. She understood that she needed to stand out from the crowd, to captivate not only with her acting skills but also with her persona. She carefully crafted her appearance, adopting a more glamorous and sophisticated style. Joan tirelessly worked to improve her posture, gestures, and speech, taking lessons from vocal coaches and movement instructors. She studied the successful actresses of the time, observing their mannerisms and learning from their performances. The transformation from Lucille LeSueur to Joan Crawford was not just a change in name but a complete reinvention. She created an identity that exuded confidence, allure, and magnetism.

Joan's determination finally caught the attention of Harry Rapf, a producer at MGM studios, in 1928. Impressed by her drive, talent, and newfound image, Rapf offered Joan a contract with the studio. It was a transformative moment in her career, as she now had the backing of a major studio. The resources, guidance, and exposure offered by MGM opened doors for her career to flourish. Joan's dedication to her craft and her willingness to adapt earned her important roles in prestigious projects, showcasing her versatility as an actress.

The journey towards becoming one of the most iconic actresses of her time had just begun. Joan Crawford's resilience, unwavering passion, and ability to adapt and reinvent herself set her on a trajectory towards greatness. Her determination to defy the odds, even in the face of rejection, illustrated her unwavering belief in her abilities. The transformation from a young girl dreaming of escaping poverty to a Hollywood star was a testament to the indomitable spirit of Joan Crawford. Little did the world know that her remarkable journey would leave an indelible mark on the history of cinema and inspire generations of aspiring actors to follow their dreams.

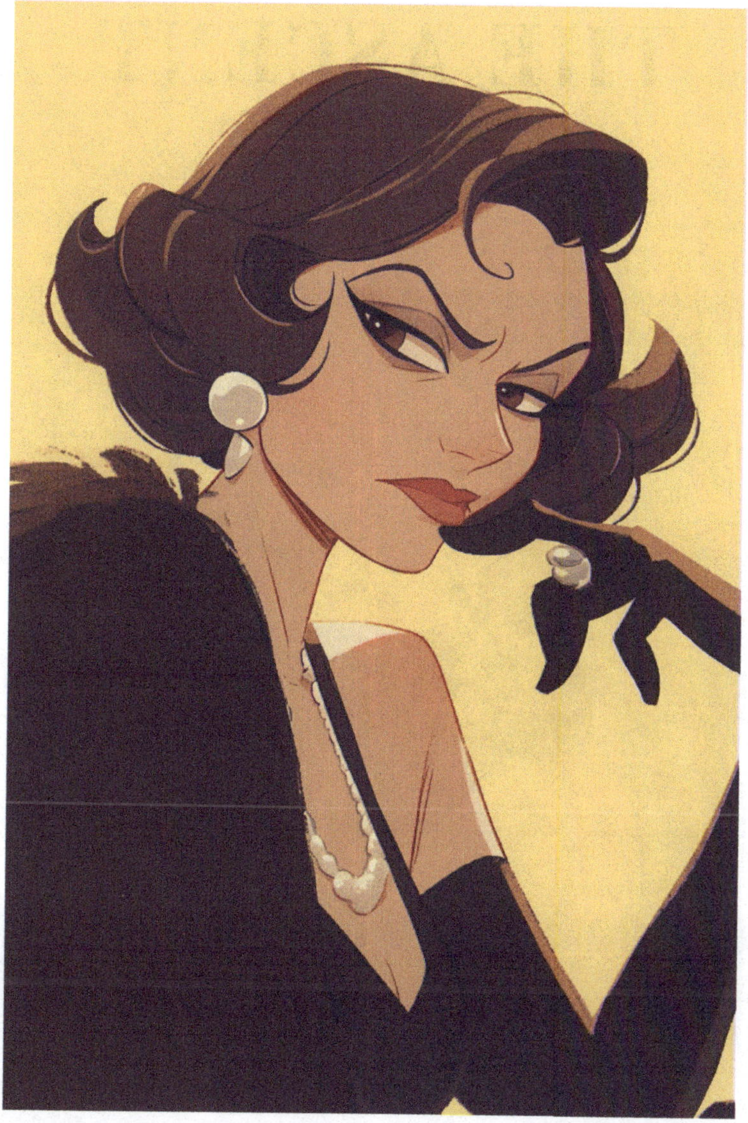

THE ASCENT BEGINS

chapter 06

Early roles and experiences in show business

Joan Crawford's journey into show business can be traced back to her humble beginnings in Texas. Determined to escape a tumultuous home environment, she left at a young age to pursue her dream of becoming an actress. This daring decision set her on a path filled with challenges, setbacks, and ultimately, an incredible success story.

As a budding artist, Crawford's initial experience onstage came in the form of chorus girl roles in various vaudeville and revue shows. These early opportunities exposed her to the world of live performance, where she learned valuable lessons in stage presence, timing, and connecting with an audience. Crawfords' dedication and work ethic quickly became evident, as she approached each show with a hunger to improve and leave a lasting impression.

It was during one of these performances that a talent scout named Harry Rapf spotted Crawford's raw talent and potential. Rapf, impressed by her dancing skills, recommended her for a small role in a silent film. This marked Crawford's entry into the world of cinema, albeit in a modest capacity.

With her first taste of filmmaking, Crawford immediately recognized the difference between acting for the stage and acting for the camera. She realized the need for subtlety, employing nuanced expressions and gestures to convey emotions that would be picked up by the lens. This newfound understanding propelled Crawford to immerse herself in acting classes and workshops, seeking guidance from experienced actors and directors.

Crawford's relentless pursuit of knowledge and her willingness to learn from others led her to collaborate with renowned directors such as Tod Browning and Clarence Brown. Under their mentorship, she gained a deeper understanding of the craft of acting, refining her skills and developing her own unique style. Browning, known for his work in horror films, taught her the art of creating tension and suspense through subtle gestures and expressions, while Brown emphasized the importance of emotional depth and authenticity.

While Crawford's talent and dedication continued to grow, she faced considerable challenges within the industry. Female performers often encountered bias, with many being seen as mere objects of beauty rather than serious actors. However, Crawford refused to be limited by these expectations. She sought out roles that allowed her to showcase her range and versatility, proving her talent and establishing herself as a serious actress.

In the face of these obstacles, Crawford's determination and ability to infuse her performances with personal experiences became her greatest strength. Despite her strive for professional success, she faced personal struggles throughout these early years. From difficulties in her personal relationships to the relentless scrutiny of the media, Crawford found solace and outlet through her work. She channeled her vulnerability, pain, and resilience into her performances, bringing an unparalleled authenticity that resonated with audiences on a profound level.

Crawford's dedication to her craft, combined with her ability to draw from her own experiences, quickly caught the attention of directors and producers. Her versatility as an actress led to her being cast in a wide range of roles, from glamorous romantic leads to complex femme fatales. With every new opportunity, Crawford left an indelible mark on the screen, captivating audiences with her captivating screen presence and emotional depth.

The early roles and experiences of Joan Crawford in show business not only shaped her as an actress but laid the foundation for her meteoric rise to stardom. From her humble beginnings as a chorus girl to her breakthrough moments on the silver screen, Crawford's dedication, resilience, and unwavering commitment to her craft set her apart from her peers. The guidance of esteemed directors, her perseverance in the face of bias, and her ability to channel personal experiences into her performances contributed to her transformation into an iconic figure of Hollywood's Golden Age.

Chapter 6 delves deep into the formative experiences and roles that shaped Joan Crawford's early years in show business. It explores her transition from the stage to the screen, the influence of mentors in refining her craft, and the personal struggles that fueled her performances. Throughout this chapter, readers will witness Crawford's evolution from a determined young woman with a dream to one of the most acclaimed and influential actresses of her time.

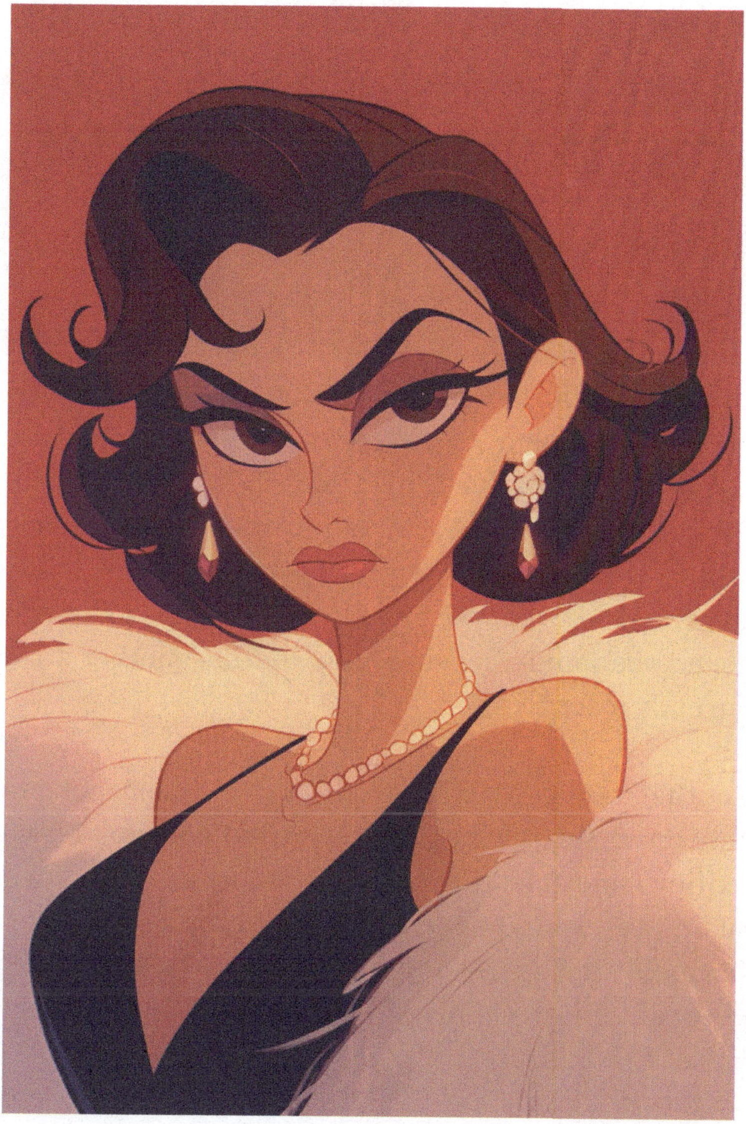

chapter 07

Transition from chorus girl to film actress

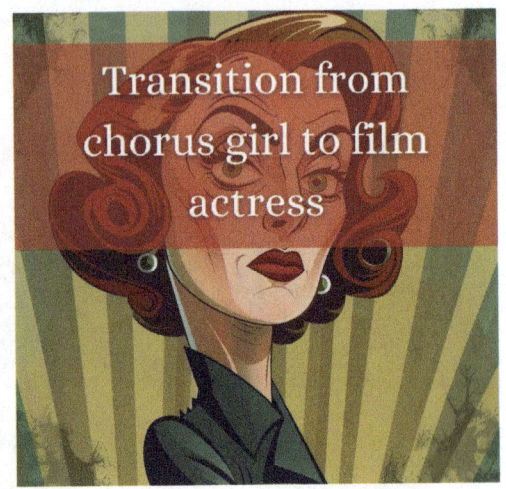

Joan Crawford's journey from a chorus girl to a renowned film actress is a testament to her perseverance and unwavering determination to succeed in Hollywood. Born Lucille Fay LeSueur on March 23, 1904, in San Antonio, Texas, Joan had a challenging childhood marked by poverty and instability. Her parents divorced when she was very young, and her father abandoned the family, leaving Joan and her mother struggling to make ends meet.

Despite the hardships she faced, Joan's dreams of stardom never wavered. As a teenager, she started entering local dance competitions and talent shows, captivating audiences with her natural grace and talent. It was during one of these performances that Joan caught the eye of a traveling theater troupe scout, who recognized her potential and offered her a position as a chorus girl.

Embracing this opportunity, Joan eagerly joined the troupe and embarked on an arduous journey across the country. The life of a chorus girl was rigorous and demanding, involving countless hours of rehearsals, performances, and constant traveling. However, Joan approached this stage of her career with an unwavering passion and an insatiable hunger for success.

In the bustling world of theater, Joan's talent shined brightly, and she quickly gained recognition for her captivating performances. Her dancing skills were unmatched, and audiences were drawn to her infectious energy and magnetic presence. It was during this time that she chose her screen name, Joan Crawford, inspired by a list of potential names she compiled after scouring newspaper headlines.

However, Joan's aspirations extended beyond the confines of the chorus line. She longed for more substantial roles and a chance to make her mark in the world of acting. Determined to expand her horizons, she took acting lessons during her personal time, honing her craft and refining her skills.

With each passing year, Joan became more determined to transition from the theater to the silver screen. She studied the works of acclaimed actors and actresses, learning from their performances and incorporating their techniques into her own. Her ambition burned brightly, and she would often gaze upon the movie posters lining the theater district, envisioning herself among the glamorous stars.

In the early 1920s, Joan's perseverance paid off. After catching the attention of a prominent film producer, she was offered a contract to appear in silent films. Overjoyed, she eagerly signed the contract, knowing that this was her chance to prove herself as a serious actress.

Joan went on to star in a series of silent films, slowly carving a niche for herself in Hollywood. Despite the challenges of silent acting, she utilized her expressive eyes and physicality to convey emotions and captivate audiences. But Joan's transformation from a chorus girl to a film actress required more than just talent—it demanded adaptability and resilience.

Transitioning from live performances to the silver screen was not without its hurdles. Joan had to learn to adjust her acting style for the camera, a medium that magnified even the smallest nuances of expression. She studied the work of acclaimed filmmakers and worked closely with directors to refine her technique. Through trial and error, she gradually mastered the art of acting for the camera, soon becoming one of the most recognized and respected actresses of the silent film era.

As the film industry transitioned into the era of "talkies," Joan faced yet another pivotal moment in her career. The introduction of synchronized sound presented new challenges and opportunities for actors. Undeterred, Joan embraced the change and adapted her acting style to incorporate her voice, immersing herself in vocal coaching and honing her delivery.

With each successful film appearance, Joan's reputation grew, paving the way for more significant roles. Directors and producers were captivated by her ability to embody diverse characters, ranging from seductive vamps to strong-willed heroines. With relentless determination, Joan asserted herself as a leading lady, often taking on powerful and complex roles that showcased her versatility as an actress.

But Joan's journey was not just one of professional success—it was also marked by personal struggles and triumphs. Off-screen, she navigated through tumultuous relationships and multiple marriages, each revealing a different layer of her complex personality. These experiences deepened her understanding of human emotions, which she infused into her performances, resonating with audiences on a profound level.

Joan's dedication to her craft was unparalleled, and she constantly sought out opportunities to challenge herself as an actress. She became known for her meticulous preparation, studying her characters inside and out to fully embody their essence. Whether it was undergoing physical transformations, intensifying her training, or delving into the psychology of her roles, Joan was always willing to go the extra mile.

Throughout her career, Joan Crawford worked alongside some of the most celebrated actors and directors of her time, leaving an indelible mark on the Golden Age of Hollywood. From her collaborations with director George Cukor in films like "A Woman's Face" (1941) and "A Star Is Born" (1954), to her powerful performances in Joseph L. Mankiewicz's "The Women" (1939) and "Mildred Pierce" (1945), Joan showcased a versatility and complexity that endeared her to audiences and critics alike.

Joan's dedication to her craft extended beyond her on-screen achievements. She tirelessly cultivated her public image, carefully crafting an aura of elegance and mystique that kept her in the spotlight even during moments of personal turmoil. With her perfectly coifed hair, impeccable fashion sense, and charismatic presence, Joan became an icon of glamour and sophistication during the height of her career.

Even as the industry evolved and new stars emerged, Joan continued to reinvent herself. From transitioning into character roles in her later years to embracing television as a medium, she embraced change instead of resisting it. Her adaptability and willingness to embrace new challenges ensured her continued relevance in the ever-changing landscape of entertainment.

Joan Crawford's transformation from a chorus girl to a celebrated film actress remains a testament to the power of determination, hard work, and an unwavering belief in oneself. Her journey serves as an inspiration for aspiring actors and actresses to never give up on their dreams, regardless of the obstacles they may face. Joan's legacy extends far beyond her filmography—it lies in her resilience, her dedication to her craft, and her constant pursuit of excellence. She will forever be remembered as a trailblazer who defied expectations and left an indelible mark on the world of entertainment.

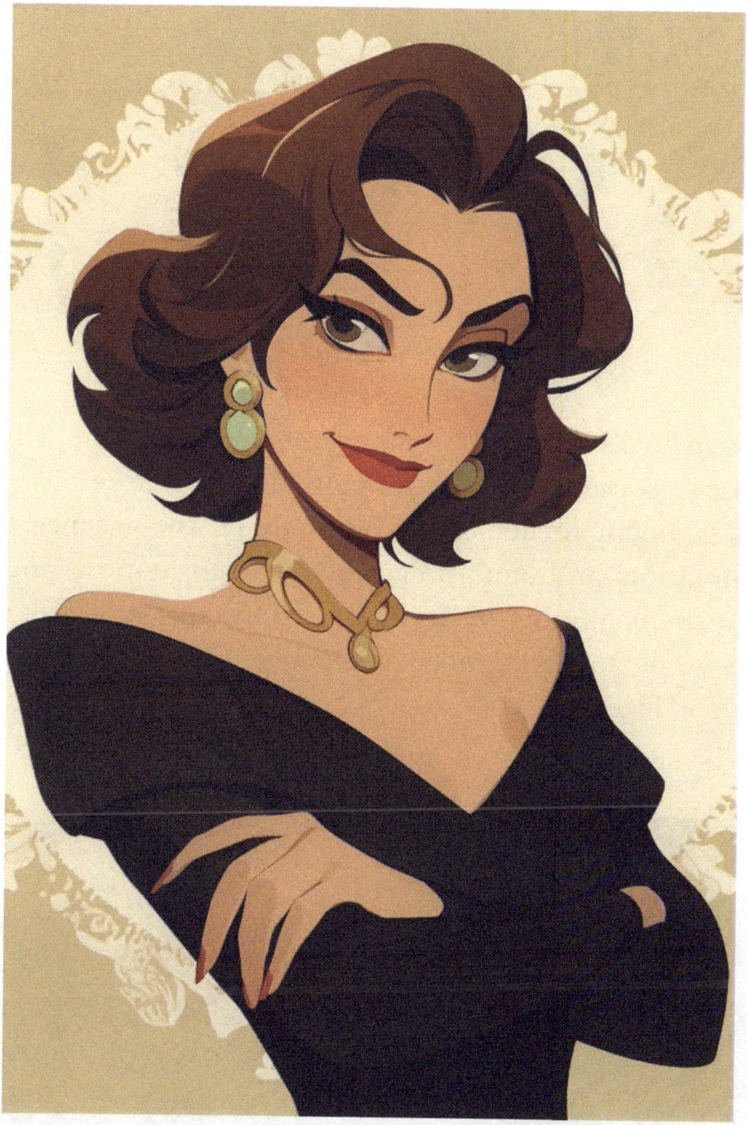

chapter 08

The significance of her name change and reinvention

Joan Crawford's decision to change her name from Lucille Fay LeSueur to something more memorable and marketable was a pivotal moment in her career, embodying the essence of her determination and ambition. This transformation not only marked the beginning of her reinvention but also set her on a path towards becoming not just a movie star, but an enduring Hollywood legend.

The process of selecting a new name was not an easy one for Joan; it required careful consideration and self-reflection. Lucille LeSueur, with its French roots, seemed too exotic for the American audience of the time. She longed for a name that would capture attention and leave an indelible mark on the collective consciousness. After much contemplation, she settled on the name "Joan Crawford."

Although seemingly simple, this name change held deeper significance for Joan. It represented a departure from her humble origins and the creation of a new, highly marketable identity. Joan Crawford became more than just a name; it became a symbol of strength, resilience, and the pursuit of the American dream. It allowed Joan to shed her past and embrace a new persona that was bold, confident, and unparalleled.

Reinvention was not just about her name; it was a complete transformation of her image, style, and persona. Joan Crawford meticulously crafted an image that encapsulated both the allure of old Hollywood glamour and the modernity of the emerging flapper era. Her fashion choices, often characterized by shoulder pads, sleek hairstyles, and couture gowns, became influential in the world of fashion. She effortlessly embodied the spirit of the times, becoming an icon of style and sophistication.

Beyond her physical appearance, Joan's reinvention extended to her acting choices, which played a crucial role in establishing her as a versatile and formidable actress. She sought out roles that were challenging, nuanced, and showcased her range. By embracing characters that were strong, independent, and commanding, she challenged the restrictive gender norms of the era and became an inspiration for women around the world.

Joan's public image was an integral part of her reinvention. She carefully cultivated an air of mystery and intrigue, maintaining a firm grip on her personal life while allowing glimpses into her glamorous world. By controlling the narrative of her relationships and engagements, she captivated the press and maintained a sense of enigma, ensuring that her personal life remained just out of reach of the public's prying eyes. With each new film and public appearance, Joan Crawford became a symbol of aspiration and fascination, an enigmatic figure whose name evoked a sense of awe and intrigue.

In retrospect, the significance of Joan Crawford's name change and reinvention cannot be understated. It became a defining moment in her career, setting her on a trajectory towards becoming one of the most enduring and celebrated stars in Hollywood history.

Her name change wasn't just an exercise in rebranding, but a symbolic gesture that represented her determination to overcome adversity and forge a new identity that would leave an indelible legacy in the annals of entertainment history. It was an act of self-reinvention that allowed her to rise above the limitations imposed by her past and transcend the expectations of her time. Through careful cultivation of her image, Joan Crawford became an embodiment of glamour, ambition, and tenacity - a beacon of hope for countless individuals striving to carve their own paths in the face of adversity.

Joan Crawford's reinvention was not without its challenges. As her star rose, she faced criticism and scrutiny from both the press and her peers. Many believed she was too ambitious, too determined to succeed. Yet, it was precisely this unwavering drive that propelled her into the realms of stardom. She refused to be defined by her past or confined to the roles assigned to women of her time. Instead, Joan Crawford reshaped her own narrative, fearlessly challenging societal norms and paving the way for future generations of women in the entertainment industry.

In conclusion, Joan Crawford's name change and subsequent reinvention were transformative moments in her career and personal life. They represented her unwavering determination, her unstoppable ambition, and her refusal to be confined by the limitations imposed on her. Through her new identity, she created a legacy that extended beyond the silver screen, serving as an inspiration to individuals around the world. Joan Crawford's name change was not just a rebranding exercise; it was the catalyst that propelled her towards unparalleled success and established her as a true Hollywood icon.

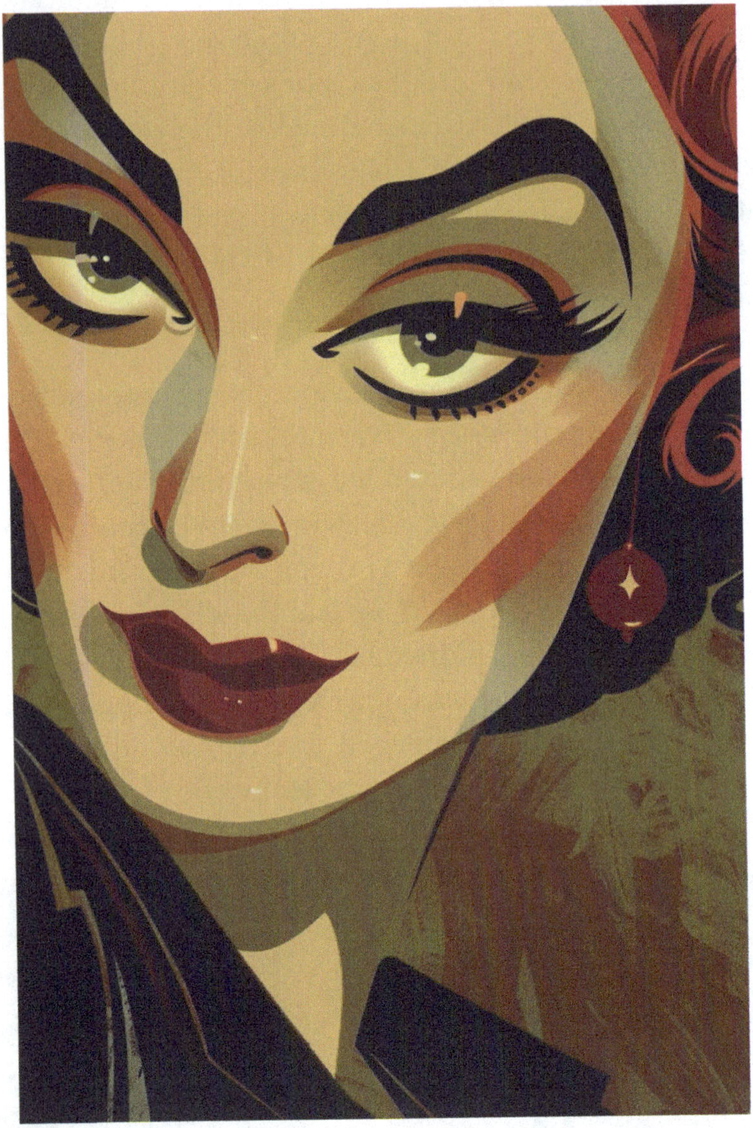

BREAKTHROUGH AND RISE TO FAME

chapter 09

Key roles and performances that catapulted her to stardom

Joan Crawford's journey to stardom was not devoid of challenges, but her talent and determination propelled her forward. This chapter delves into the key roles and performances that played a crucial role in catapulting her to stardom. These milestones not only showcased her acting prowess but also solidified her position as one of Hollywood's leading actresses.

One of the earliest influential roles in Joan Crawford's career was her performance in the 1928 silent film "Our Dancing Daughters." The film, directed by Harry Beaumont, followed the lives of three young women in the Jazz Age. Crawford played the vivacious and rebellious character of Diana Medford, a young flapper who defied societal norms and reveled in the pleasures of the time. Her portrayal captivated audiences, as her energy and charisma radiated off the screen. The film not only established Crawford's image as the epitome of the 1920s flapper but also showcased her ability to embody the spirit of an era marked by social changes and female empowerment. "Our Dancing Daughters" became a box office success, making Crawford a rising star in Hollywood.

Another significant role that contributed to Crawford's rise to stardom was her portrayal of Sadie Thompson in the 1928 film "Sadie Thompson." Directed by Raoul Walsh, this film was an adaptation of W. Somerset Maugham's play "Rain." In "Sadie Thompson," Crawford played the title character, a free-spirited woman whose life takes a dramatic turn when she clashes with a zealous missionary in Samoa. Crawford's dynamic performance as the morally complex protagonist earned her critical acclaim. She effectively depicted Sadie Thompson's vulnerability and strength, as well as the internal struggles she faced due to societal judgement and expectations. Her role in "Sadie Thompson" showcased her ability to navigate the nuances of her character, drawing sympathy and empathy from the audience. It marked a turning point in her career, solidifying her as a serious actress capable of delivering compelling performances. Moreover, the film marked her successful transition from silent films to the talkie era, displaying her adaptability as an actress.

Crawford continued to demonstrate her range and versatility through her role in the 1932 film "Grand Hotel." Directed by Edmund Goulding, the film boasted an ensemble cast that included Greta Garbo and John Barrymore. Crawford played the character of Flaemmchen, a struggling stenographer who aspired to be an actress. Her performance stood out amidst the star-studded cast, displaying not only her natural beauty and magnetic screen presence but also her ability to bring depth and vulnerability to her role. Flaemmchen's journey resonated with audiences, and Crawford's portrayal made her character relatable and endearing. "Grand Hotel" became a critical and commercial success, further elevating Crawford's status as an actress who could hold her own among Hollywood's elite.

However, it was the 1945 film "Mildred Pierce" that stands as one of Joan Crawford's most memorable performances. Directed by Michael Curtiz and based on James M. Cain's novel of the same name, the film follows the story of Mildred Pierce, a determined single mother who opens a restaurant to provide for her daughters. Crawford's portrayal of Mildred Pierce showcased her ability to balance strength and vulnerability, making the character multidimensional and compelling. She expertly navigated Mildred's journey through sacrifice, motherhood, and betrayal against the backdrop of a murder mystery. Crawford's emotional depth and commitment to her character earned her universal critical acclaim. Her performance in "Mildred Pierce" earned her an Academy Award for Best Actress, solidifying her status as one of Hollywood's leading ladies. Beyond her on-screen talent, Crawford's fierce determination and work ethic played a significant role in the success of "Mildred Pierce" and showcased her continued dedication to her craft throughout her career.

In addition to these key roles, Joan Crawford had several other notable performances throughout her career. In the pre-Code era, she delivered standout performances in films like "Dance, Fools, Dance" (1931), where she played a young woman caught between two brothers involved in criminal activities, "Possessed" (1931), where she portrayed a woman descending into madness due to an obsessive love, and "Rain" (1932), where she brought the tragic character of Sadie Thompson to life once again. These films showcased her ability to tackle complex and challenging roles, often portraying women who defied societal expectations. Her emotional depth and commitment to her characters allowed her to imbue these roles with a sense of realism that resonated with audiences.

In 1939, Crawford starred in "The Women," a comedy-drama directed by George Cukor. The film, adapted from Clare Boothe Luce's play, depicted the lives of wealthy Manhattan socialites. In "The Women," Crawford played the role of Crystal Allen, a glamorous and assertive perfume saleswoman who becomes involved in a love triangle. While not the lead role, Crawford's portrayal captivated attention, as she brought charisma and magnetism to a character who challenged traditional gender roles. Crystal Allen showcased Crawford's ability to embody strong-willed and nuanced characters, leaving a lasting impression on the audience.

Perhaps one of the most iconic roles of Joan Crawford's later career came in the 1962 film "What Ever Happened to Baby Jane?" Directed by Robert Aldrich, this psychological thriller paired Crawford with her long-time rival Bette Davis, creating a highly anticipated on-screen clash. In the film, Crawford portrayed the character of Blanche Hudson, a former actress locked in a deteriorating relationship with her unstable sister, played by Davis. The film pushed both actresses to their limits, with Crawford delivering a commanding and haunting performance that resonated with audiences. Although overshadowed by Davis's ferocious portrayal, Crawford's portrayal of Blanche showcased her ability to convey vulnerability, fear, and a crumbling sense of identity. "What Ever Happened to Baby Jane?" revived Crawford's career and demonstrated her resilience and commitment to her craft even in the face of personal and professional challenges.

Through these pivotal roles, Joan Crawford established her reputation as a talented and versatile actress, which ultimately led to her enduring stardom. From her early flapper roles to her riveting portrayals of complex women, Crawford captivated audiences with her emotional range, sophistication, and captivating presence on screen. Each performance showcased her dedication to her craft and her ability to bring depth, complexity, and relatability to her characters. Joan Crawford's impact on the film industry goes beyond her stellar performances. Her fierce determination, unwavering work ethic, and enduring legacy continue to inspire generations of actors and filmmakers, cementing her status as a true Hollywood icon.

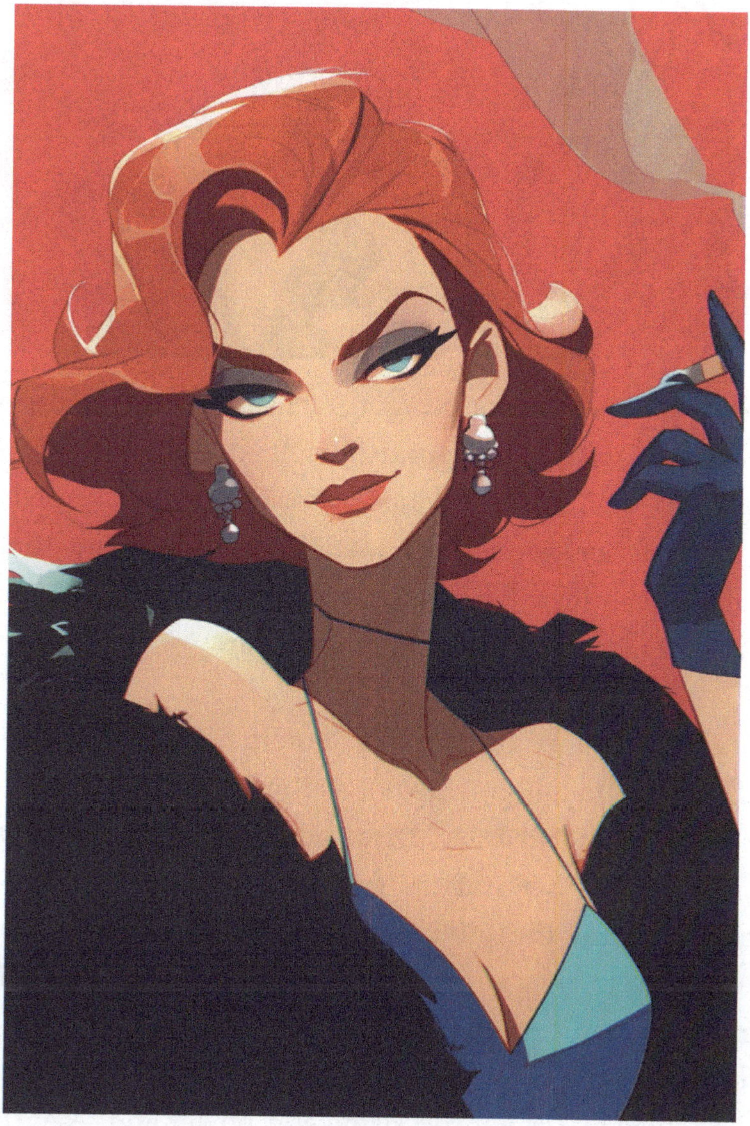

chapter 10

Behind-the-scenes stories of her breakthrough films

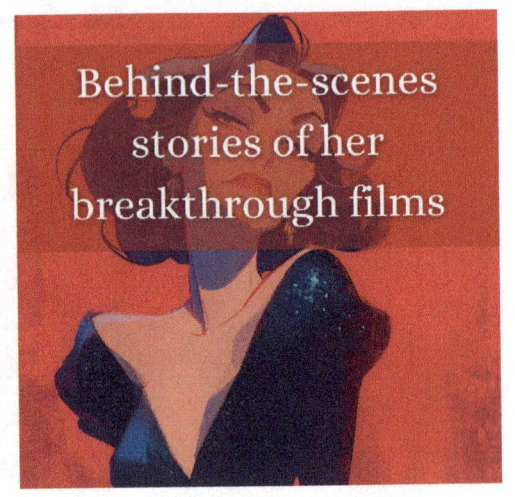

As Joan Crawford's career began to soar in the early years of her Hollywood journey, she found herself at the center of some remarkable behind-the-scenes stories that shaped the trajectory of her success. It was during this time that she starred in a series of breakthrough films that solidified her place as one of the industry's brightest stars.

One of the most intriguing stories emerges from the making of "Our Dancing Daughters" (1928), a film that marked a turning point in Crawford's career. Directed by Harry Beaumont, the film showcased her talent for both dancing and acting. However, behind the glitz and glamour, tensions simmered between Crawford and her co-star, Anita Page. While their on-screen chemistry sizzled, the off-screen relationship was marked by jealousy and competing ambitions. Page felt overshadowed by Crawford's rising star power and resented the attention she garnered. Despite their differences, the film was a commercial and critical success, propelling both actresses into the limelight. It served as a testament to Crawford's ability to captivate audiences, even amidst personal conflicts.

Another fascinating behind-the-scenes moment occurred during the filming of "Grand Hotel" (1932), a star-studded MGM production featuring an ensemble cast that included Greta Garbo, John Barrymore, and Wallace Beery. Crawford's role as the ambitious stenographer, Flaemmchen, brought her character to life with a magnetic intensity. However, it was her on-screen pairing with John Barrymore that set the screen ablaze. Their electrifying chemistry caught the attention of audiences, making them question whether the sparks were merely on-screen or if a real-life love affair was brewing. Rumors of a passionate romance fueled the film's allure, and the public's fascination with their alleged relationship only served to enhance Crawford's star status. In reality, Crawford and Barrymore shared a deeply professional admiration and respect, ensuring their captivating performances were a testament to their undeniable talent.

In 1945, Crawford starred in "Mildred Pierce," a film that not only showcased her immense acting abilities but also marked a significant milestone in her career. Based on James M. Cain's novel, "Mildred Pierce" saw Crawford bring the resilient and determined title character to life. Behind the scenes, this film held immense personal significance. Crawford saw Mildred Pierce as an opportunity to break away from her glamorous image and prove her versatility as an actress. She committed fully to the character, immersing herself in research and drawing from her own personal experiences to shape Mildred's emotional journey.

To prepare for the role, Crawford spent time observing working-class women, studying their mannerisms, and understanding their struggles. She even took home economics classes to master the art of cooking, enabling her to authentically portray Mildred's transformation from a humble waitress to a successful businesswoman. Crawford's dedication to the role mirrored her own life experiences, as she too had overcome hurdles to achieve her success in Hollywood.

Crawford's collaboration with director Michael Curtiz was instrumental in translating her dedication into a layered and memorable portrayal. Curtiz's meticulous attention to detail and insistence on multiple takes pushed Crawford to dig deeper into her character's psyche. Their partnership resulted in a performance filled with raw emotion and a level of authenticity that resonated with audiences.

When "Mildred Pierce" was released, it became an instant success. Crawford's portrayal of the determined and ultimately tragic Mildred captivated audiences and critics alike. The film's success was a testament to her talent, earning her the Academy Award for Best Actress. This accolade served as a validation of her triumph over adversity and her transformation within the industry. It showcased Crawford's ability to transcend her glamorous image and delve into complex, nuanced roles that were grounded in truth.

"The Women" (1939) presented another noteworthy behind-the-scenes story. As an all-female cast worked under the guidance of director George Cukor, Crawford found herself surrounded by formidable actresses such as Norma Shearer, Rosalind Russell, and Joan Fontaine. The film depicted the lives and relationships of women in New York high society, with Crawford portraying the tenacious Crystal Allen. Despite fierce competition for the limelight, these women formed a unique bond on and off the set.

Crawford's collaboration with Cukor allowed her to tap into her versatility, showcasing a depth of emotions and razor-sharp wit. She brought her own brand of strength and vulnerability to the character, making Crystal Allen more than just a conniving antagonist. Crawford's portrayal brought nuance and complexity to a role that could have easily been one-dimensional. The film's success was a testament to the talent and camaraderie that existed among the actresses, proving that women could dominate the screen and deliver powerful performances.

These are just a few examples of the fascinating behind-the-scenes stories of Joan Crawford's breakthrough films. Each movie represented a pivotal moment in her career, where her dedication, talent, and determination converged to create unforgettable performances. Through the battles and triumphs of these films, Crawford proved herself to be not just a stunning presence on the silver screen, but also a consummate professional who left an indelible mark on the history of Hollywood.

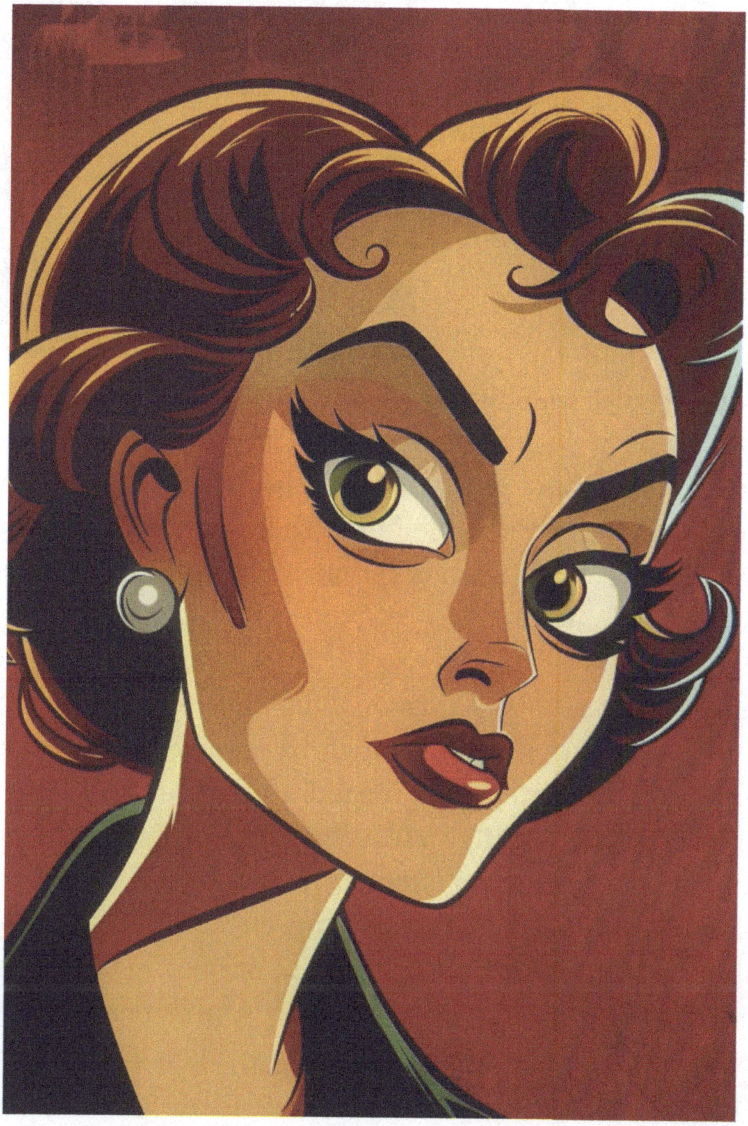

chapter 11

The impact of her success on her personal life

Joan Crawford's meteoric rise to fame had a profound and complex impact on her personal life, transforming it in ways she never could have imagined. As she ascended the ranks of Hollywood, fame and fortune found their way into every corner of her existence, leaving an indelible mark on her relationships, lifestyle, and identity.

One of the most notable impacts of her success was the strain it put on her relationships. Crawford's relentless pursuit of stardom often left little room for maintaining close connections with friends and family. The demands of her career took priority, and she found herself constantly on the move, shooting films, attending events, and engaging in promotional activities. While she cherished the support of her inner circle, the pressures of her newfound celebrity status tested the limits of those relationships and her ability to balance her personal and professional life.

Her first marriage to actor Douglas Fairbanks Jr. began to crumble under the weight of their respective careers. Both struggling to navigate their own rising stardom, their relationship became strained, filled with competing priorities and the challenges of maintaining a sense of independence in the face of overwhelming public demand. The couple often found themselves caught up in the whirlwind of their separate careers, leaving little time for nurturing their bond. Arguments became commonplace, exacerbated by the pressures of fame and the constant exposure to outside influences. In the end, they both realized that their individual ambitions and the sacrifices required to achieve them were irreconcilable with the needs of their marriage.

Crawford's pursuit of success deeply impacted her relationship with her children as well. Her demanding schedule left little time for quality bonding with her daughters, Christina and Cathy. While she deeply loved and cared for her children, her drive for success often left them longing for more of her presence and attention. The burden of being raised by a famous mother created a unique set of challenges for the girls, who sought solace and stability in their own ways amidst the whirlwind of their mother's career. This dynamic later became the subject of Christina's controversial memoir, "Mommie Dearest," which depicted Crawford as an abusive and neglectful parent. The book exposed the harsh realities of their relationship and added another layer of strain to their already complicated family dynamics.

The impact of her success on her personal life extended beyond relationships as well. Crawford's ever-growing wealth and stardom afforded her a luxurious lifestyle that few could imagine. She indulged in extravagant parties, lavish homes, and a wardrobe filled with designer garments. The opulence of her surroundings became synonymous with her image and allowed her to project a sense of elegance and prosperity. However, the pursuit and maintenance of this lavish lifestyle often came at the expense of personal happiness and inner peace. Beneath the surface of this apparent grandeur, Joan struggled with feelings of emptiness and a constant need to prove her worth, driving her to continually seek external validation.

As her star continued to rise, Crawford's personal life became a spectacle for the public to dissect. With her every move captured and scrutinized, rumors and scandals dominated newspaper headlines, further complicating her attempts to maintain a sense of privacy. Whether it was whispers of tumultuous affairs, dramatic feuds with co-stars, or the strain within her family, her status as a Hollywood icon left her vulnerable to the prying eyes and judgment of the public. This constant scrutiny weighed heavily on her mental and emotional well-being, forcing her to navigate a delicate balance between satisfying her fans' expectations and preserving her own sense of self.

Despite these challenges, Crawford's success also brought her immense personal fulfillment. The love and adoration she received from fans fueled her ambition and kept her motivated to reach even greater heights. She found solace in her work and the joy it brought to others, knowing that she had achieved a level of success that few could ever dream of. At times, the applause and admiration became an affirmation of her worth and a salve for the sacrifices she made along her journey to stardom. However, even amidst the accolades, there was a constant battle to reconcile the external recognition with her internal struggles, as her personal happiness and the elusive quest for contentment often remained just out of reach.

In conclusion, the impact of Joan Crawford's success on her personal life was a complex interplay of triumphs and sacrifices. While it brought her wealth, fame, and personal fulfillment, it also strained her relationships, subjected her to intense public scrutiny, and required her to navigate the intricate dance between her public image and private self. The magnitude of her success demanded relentless commitment, resilience, and an unwavering determination to prevail, adding layers of complexity to her journey through fame and leaving an indelible mark on her personal narrative. The path to stardom may have brought her a measure of happiness, yet the cost of that success reverberated throughout her personal life, leaving Crawford forever entangled in the paradoxes of fame.

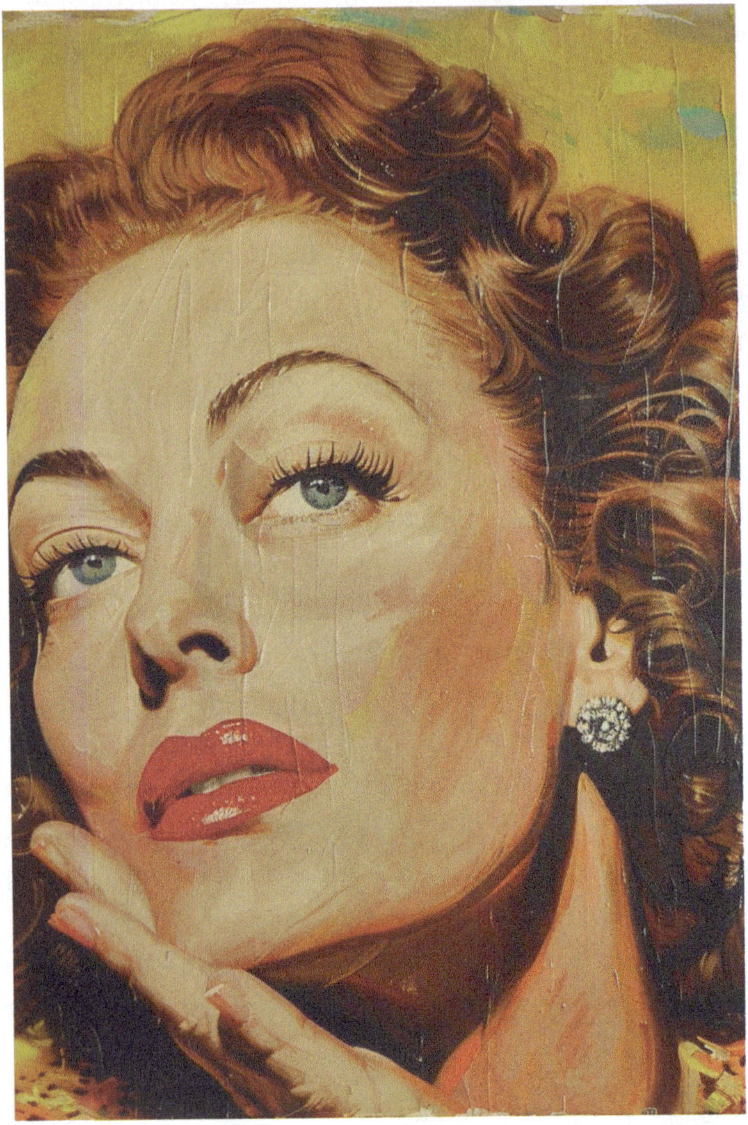

ICON OF THE SILVER SCREEN

chapter 12

Analysis of her most iconic roles and performances

Joan Crawford's illustrious career as a film actress spanned several decades, leaving behind a legacy of unforgettable characters and performances. Through her dynamic portrayals, Crawford showcased her versatility as an actress, bringing depth and complexity to a wide range of roles. In this chapter, we will delve deeper into some of her most iconic performances, exploring the reasons behind their enduring legacy and the impact they had on both the film industry and society as a whole.

One of Crawford's most iconic roles was that of Mildred Pierce in the 1945 film of the same name, based on James M. Cain's novel. Directed by Michael Curtiz, this film showcased Crawford's ability to inhabit the depths of a character's emotional journey. As Mildred, she brilliantly conveyed a determined and hardworking woman who is willing to do whatever it takes to provide for her family. Crawford flawlessly captured the complexities of the character, showcasing Mildred's unwavering strength and ambition, as well as her vulnerability in matters of the heart. Her fearless and heartfelt portrayal earned her an Academy Award for Best Actress, solidifying her position as one of Hollywood's leading ladies and inspiring a new generation of actresses who admired her ability to portray strong, multifaceted women.

Another notable performance by Joan Crawford came in the 1939 film "The Women," directed by George Cukor. In this all-female cast, Crawford portrayed Crystal Allen, a seductive and cunning showgirl who becomes the catalyst for turmoil among a circle of affluent women. Crawford's portrayal of Crystal exuded a charismatic confidence, blending allure with a hint of duplicity. She brought a sense of complexity and depth to the character, making Crystal more than just a typical "other woman" trope. Crawford's ability to effortlessly embody a femme fatale character was captivating, demonstrating her commanding screen presence and her talent for portraying complex roles that challenged societal expectations of women.

In 1947, Crawford starred in "Possessed," a psychological drama that allowed her to showcase her range and ability to portray intense emotions. Directed by Curtis Bernhardt, the film follows the tumultuous journey of Louise Howell, a woman grappling with obsession and emotional instability. Crawford's portrayal was raw, poignant, and haunting as she masterfully portrayed the torment and fragility of her character. She captivated audiences with her ability to bring the internal struggles of Louise to life, delivering a performance that was both mesmerizing and deeply human. Her nuanced portrayal earned her yet another Academy Award nomination, further solidifying her reputation as a formidable actress who could breathe life into complex characters.

However, one cannot discuss Joan Crawford's most iconic roles without mentioning her performance in the 1962 film "What Ever Happened to Baby Jane?" Directed by Robert Aldrich, this psychological horror-thriller paired Crawford with fellow Hollywood legend Bette Davis. As the mentally unstable former child star Blanche Hudson, Crawford delivered a captivating performance that was both chilling and sympathetic. Throughout the film, Crawford masterfully balanced the delicate line between vulnerability and madness, capturing the tragic and twisted nature of her character. Her portrayal of Blanche encapsulated the fears of aging and the psychological turmoil that can exist within familial relationships. With her skilled portrayal, she crafted a compelling narrative that shocked audiences and challenged traditional Hollywood expectations, paving the way for psychological thrillers to explore dynamic female characters in a unique and powerful manner.

Joan Crawford's talent for breathing life into complex characters not only entertained audiences but also pushed the boundaries of gender roles and challenged societal norms. Throughout her career, she brought stories to the screen that showcased the multidimensional experiences of women, exploring their struggles, ambitions, and the complexities of their emotions. Her performances resonated deeply with viewers, inspiring a new generation of actors and filmmakers to create narratives that were more representative of the diverse female experience.

In the following chapters, we will continue to explore the impact and legacy of Joan Crawford's life and career, delving into her personal and professional choices that made her an enduring Hollywood icon. We will examine her philanthropic endeavors, her influence on fashion and style, and the lasting impression she left on the film industry as a whole.

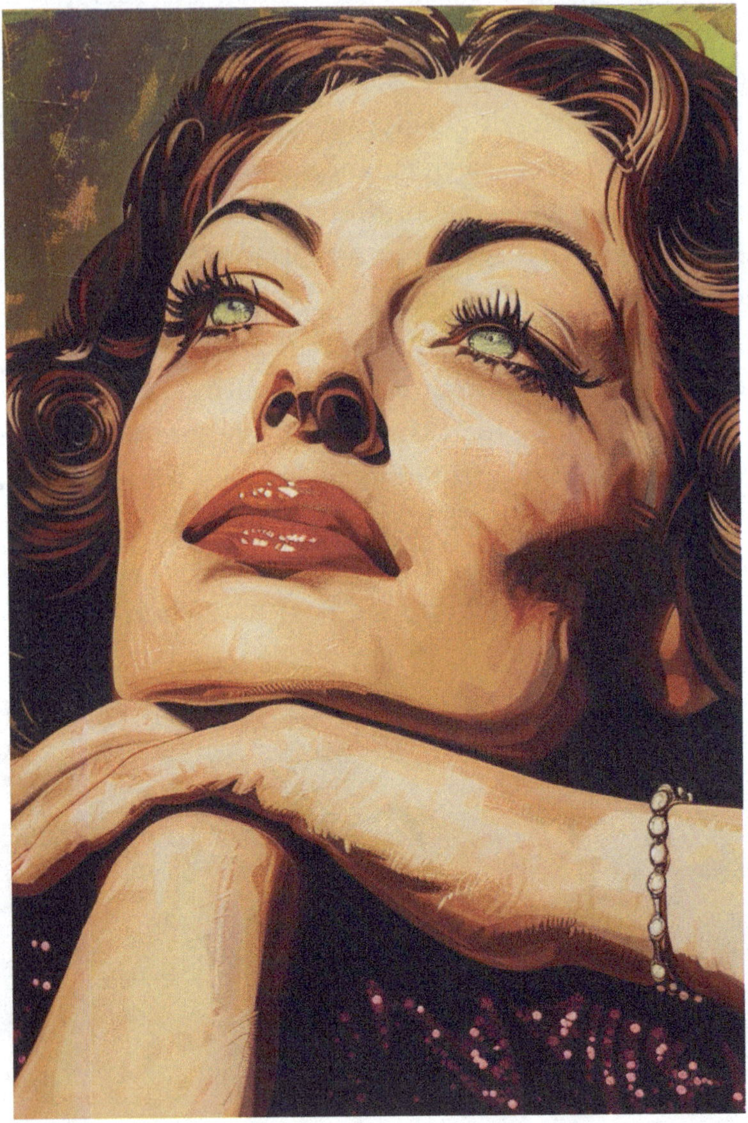

chapter 13

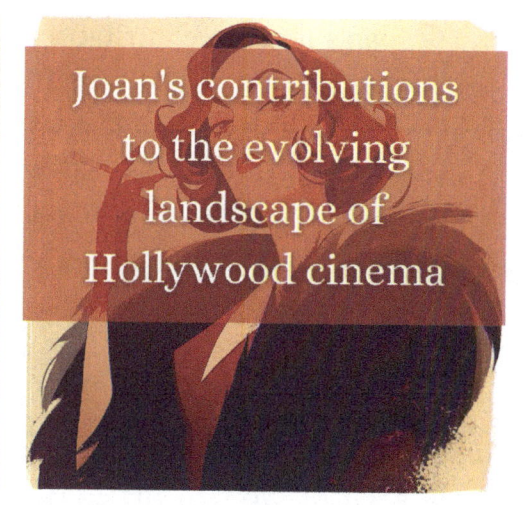

Joan's contributions to the evolving landscape of Hollywood cinema

In the midst of a rapidly evolving Hollywood, Joan Crawford emerged as not only a leading actress but also a trailblazer who left an indelible mark on the film industry. Her contributions spanned various aspects of cinema, from her performances to her involvement behind the scenes.

One of Joan's notable contributions was her ability to adapt to the changing tides of Hollywood. Throughout her career, she demonstrated a remarkable versatility that allowed her to effortlessly transition from silent films to talkies, and later embrace the transition to color films. This adaptability showcased not only her talent but also her willingness to evolve with the medium and stay relevant in an industry that was constantly changing.

Furthermore, Joan played a pivotal role in challenging the stereotypes of women in Hollywood. At a time when most female characters were portrayed as damsels in distress, Joan consistently sought out roles that defied these conventions. Her characters often exhibited strength, ambition, and assertiveness, breaking the mold of how women were typically portrayed onscreen. Through her performances, Joan paved the way for future actresses to delve into complex and multifaceted roles, encouraging the industry to recognize the depth and versatility of female talent.

Joan's influence extended beyond her acting prowess; she left an indelible mark on the business side of the film industry. Recognizing the importance of branding and image, she carefully crafted her public persona, becoming one of the first actors to actively involve herself in self-promotion. Joan understood the power of the media and actively worked with publicity teams to create and maintain her image, which, in turn, boosted her career and helped her remain a top star in the industry. She strategically controlled her narrative, carefully selecting the roles she took on and even going as far as changing her name early in her career to project a more glamorous and alluring image.

Additionally, Joan had a significant impact on the production side of filmmaking. In 1943, she founded her own production company, Joan Crawford Productions, which allowed her greater creative control over her projects. This move not only demonstrated her entrepreneurial spirit but also provided a platform for her to champion stories she believed in. Through her production company, Joan collaborated with emerging talent and brought lesser-known stories to the silver screen, further contributing to the diversity of narratives in Hollywood. Her determination to tell meaningful stories and the risks she took in supporting emerging talent marked her as a true industry innovator.

Beyond her individual contributions, Joan Crawford's impact on Hollywood cinema can be seen in the lasting influence she has had on future generations of actors and filmmakers. Her dedication to her craft, unwavering commitment to her image, and fearless approach to pushing boundaries have inspired countless artists to strive for greatness. From her iconic roles, such as the enduring "Mildred Pierce," to her business acumen, Joan's legacy continues to shape the evolving landscape of Hollywood cinema.

Furthermore, Joan was a trailblazer when it came to advocating for fair treatment and better working conditions for actors. Recognizing the exploitative nature of studio contracts and the lack of creative control, she fought for the rights of actors to have more agency in their careers. In 1947, she joined forces with other Hollywood stars, including Bette Davis, to form the first-ever celebrity-backed labor union, the Screen Actors Guild (SAG). Through her involvement in SAG, Joan tirelessly lobbied for better wages, improved working hours, and protection against unfair treatment by the studios. Her efforts not only benefited actors during her time but also laid the foundation for the rights and protections actors enjoy today.

Moreover, Joan's commitment to community building within the industry extended beyond SAG. She actively mentored and nurtured emerging talent, recognizing the importance of supporting the next generation of actors and filmmakers. Through her production company, Joan provided opportunities for up-and-coming actors and writers, often showcasing their talent in her films. This collaborative and supportive approach to filmmaking created a sense of camaraderie and mentorship that shaped Hollywood's landscape, instilling a value for fostering talent and nurturing artistic growth.

Joan's impact on Hollywood extended to her timeless sense of style, which continues to inspire fashion trends and captivate audiences. With her impeccable taste and glamorous allure, she became a fashion icon, influencing both on and off-screen fashion trends. From her signature broad-shouldered dresses to her perfectly coiffed hair, Joan set the standard for elegance and sophistication, leaving an indelible mark on the world of fashion.

As we delve deeper into Joan Crawford's career, it becomes evident that her contributions were far-reaching and left an indelible mark on the film industry. Her talent, resilience, determination, and commitment to social causes paved the way for future generations and redefined what it means to be a Hollywood star. Joan's captivating performances, business savvy, philanthropy, and empowerment of others through mentorship ensure that her legacy remains relevant and celebrated, making her an enduring icon in the history of film.

From challenging traditional gender roles to actively participating in her self-promotion, Joan Crawford's influence went beyond acting, extending to reshaping the very nature of Hollywood itself. She left an indelible mark on the industry, not only as an actress but also as a leader and a voice for change. Her contributions continue to inspire contemporary filmmakers, actors, and viewers, encouraging them to challenge norms, embrace innovation, and strive for excellence. Joan's presence in Hollywood cinema will forever be cherished, honoring her as a true icon of the silver screen.

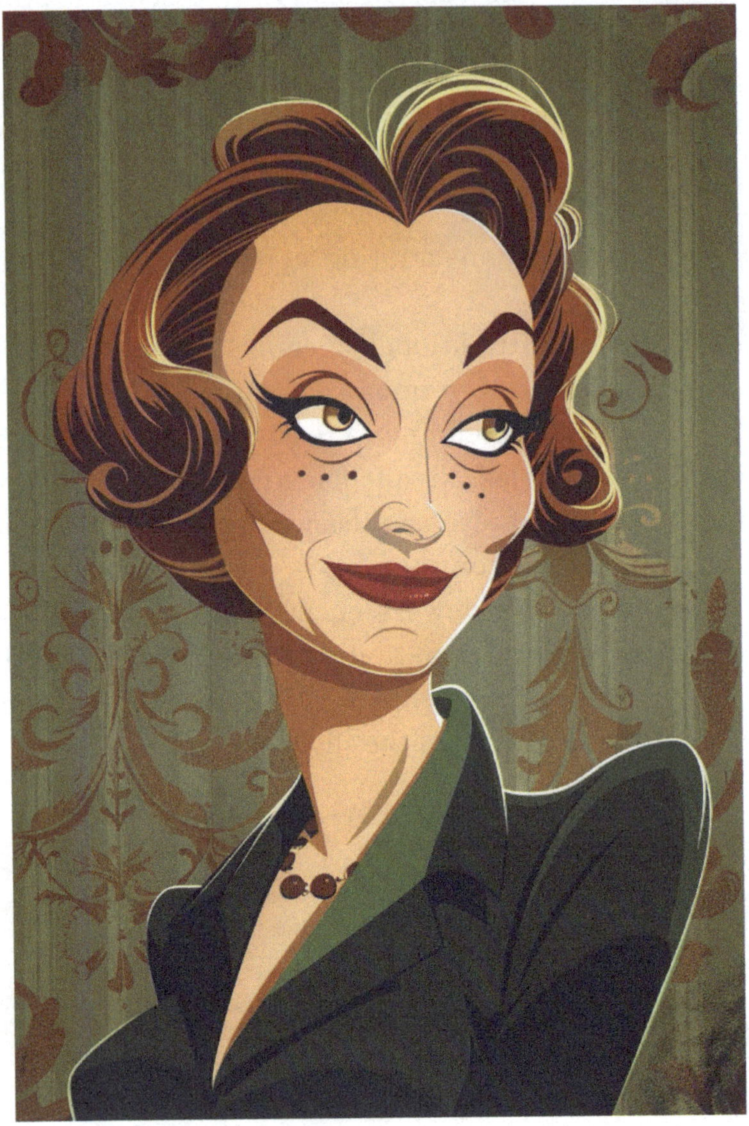

Chapter 14

Critical acclaim and public reception

Throughout her illustrious career, Joan Crawford received a considerable amount of critical acclaim and public reception. Her performances on screen were often praised for their depth, intensity, and versatility, cementing her status as one of the greatest actresses of her time.

Crawford's versatility as an actress extended beyond the characters she portrayed; it was evident in the genres she explored. From thrilling dramas to romantic comedies, she effortlessly transitioned between various roles, showcasing her adaptability and range. This ability to inhabit different personas allowed her to captivate audiences across a wide spectrum of films and solidified her as a true chameleon of the silver screen.

One of her most critically acclaimed performances came in the 1945 film "Mildred Pierce," directed by Michael Curtiz. In this noir drama, Crawford played the title character, a determined mother who becomes a successful businesswoman in order to provide for her family. The poignancy and vulnerability she brought to the role earned her an Academy Award for Best Actress, establishing her as a force to be reckoned with in the industry. The film's success further solidified Crawford's reputation as a skilled actress who could command the screen with her presence.

While "Mildred Pierce" is often regarded as Crawford's pinnacle achievement, it is important to recognize the breadth and depth of her filmography. Her early roles in silent films, such as "Our Dancing Daughters" (1928), showcased her natural grace and beauty. As the talkies emerged, Crawford effortlessly transitioned, showcasing her talent in films like "Rain" (1932), where she played Sadie Thompson, a free-spirited prostitute trying to find redemption in a South Seas island.

Beyond her dramatic roles, Crawford also excelled in comedies, displaying a flair for timing and delivering sharp dialogue. In films like "The Women" (1939) and "A Woman's Face" (1941), Crawford showcased her comedic talents, delivering memorable performances that balanced humor with poignancy. This versatility enabled her to appeal to a wide range of audiences and solidify her status as a bankable star.

One of the reasons Crawford's performances resonated so deeply with audiences was her dedication to preparation and authenticity. Known for her meticulous approach to her roles, she would immerse herself in the lives of her characters, thoroughly researching their backgrounds and mannerisms. She insisted on extensive rehearsals and would often collaborate closely with directors to ensure the best possible portrayal. This commitment to her craft allowed her to bring a depth and emotional truth to her performances that audiences found captivating and relatable.

Throughout her career, Crawford also faced criticism from some quarters. Some argued that her acting style was too melodramatic and that she relied too heavily on emotional intensity rather than subtlety. However, it can be argued that Crawford's emotional intensity was precisely what made her performances stand out. She had an unparalleled ability to tap into a character's deepest emotions, bringing them to the surface in a way that resonated with audiences. Her raw and powerful performances allowed viewers to empathize with her characters and become emotionally invested in their stories.

Public reception of Crawford was complex, as she became both a beloved icon and a subject of speculation and controversy. Her private life, marked by multiple marriages and personal upheavals, often overshadowed her professional achievements. However, her dedication to her craft and her unwavering commitment to giving her best performance remained a constant source of admiration for her fans. Despite the ups and downs of her personal life, people were captivated by her ability to deliver stellar performances time and time again.

Even after her retirement from acting in the 1970s, Joan Crawford's impact on popular culture remained significant. Her iconic persona, style, and dedication to her career set the stage for future generations of actresses. Many current actors cite Crawford as a source of inspiration and a trailblazer in the industry, honoring her influence on the craft. Her legacy extends beyond her on-screen achievements, as she proved that with talent, determination, and resilience, one can overcome personal struggles and leave an indelible mark on the entertainment industry.

In conclusion, Joan Crawford's performances consistently garnered critical acclaim and captivated the public. Her ability to bring depth and emotional authenticity to her characters secured her a place among Hollywood's finest. While she faced both praise and criticism, her enduring legacy as a talented actress and cultural icon underlines her impact on the entertainment industry. Her ability to transcend boundaries and connect with audiences on a profound level is a testament to her exceptional talent and enduring legacy. Joan Crawford's contributions to the art of acting will continue to inspire generations to come, reminding us of the power of storytelling and the unyielding spirit of those who pursue their passion.

chatvariety.com

THE WOMAN BEHIND THE LEGEND

chapter 15

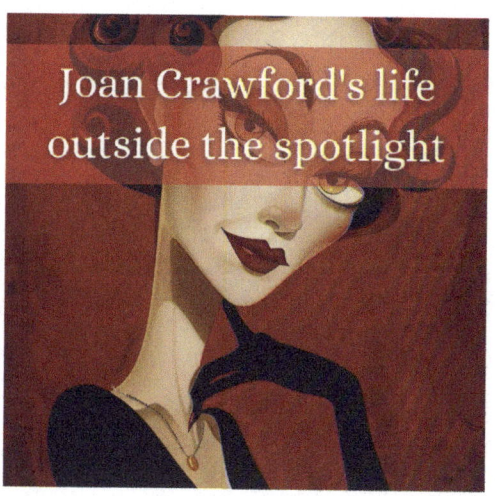

Joan Crawford's life outside the spotlight

As one of the most glamorous and iconic stars of Hollywood's golden age, Joan Crawford's life in the public eye was filled with drama, success, and adoration. However, behind the scenes, she lived a life that was just as fascinating and complex.

Outside of her illustrious career, Joan Crawford led a private life marked by personal relationships, marriages, and family obligations. Over the years, she had four husbands, each contributing to different chapters of her life. Crawford's first marriage to actor Douglas Fairbanks Jr., an influential figure in the industry, provided her with an entryway into Tinseltown's elite circles. However, their union was short-lived, ending after only three years due to conflicting personalities and career ambitions.

Following her divorce from Fairbanks, Crawford embarked on an intense and tempestuous relationship with fellow actor Franchot Tone. Their love affair began on the set of the film "Today We Live" in 1933 and quickly became the talk of Hollywood. Their on-screen chemistry translated into a passionate romance, leading to marriage in 1935. While their love for each other was undeniable, their frequent clashes and discordant lifestyles strained their marriage. Crawford's immense dedication to her career often collided with Tone's more laid-back approach. Additionally, Tone's struggle with alcoholism added strain to the relationship, ultimately leading to their divorce in 1939.

In 1942, Crawford married actor Phillip Terry, with whom she had two children. The marriage provided her with a sense of stability and domesticity that she had long craved. However, as their careers began to diverge, tensions arose. Crawford's rising stardom often led to extended periods of separation from Terry, affecting their relationship. Despite their amicable relationship, their marriage ended in 1946. Both Crawford and Terry ultimately remarried and found happiness in their respective relationships.

Crawford's fourth and final marriage was to Alfred Steele, then CEO of PepsiCo. Their union in 1955 not only solidified her as a high-profile power couple but also introduced Crawford to the world of business and corporate influence. Steele's business acumen and guidance propelled Crawford into a new chapter of her career. During her marriage to Steele, Crawford became heavily involved in PepsiCo's marketing and advertising campaigns, contributing to the company's success and further expanding Crawford's own business ventures.

Beyond her personal relationships and family obligations, Joan Crawford was also deeply committed to philanthropic endeavors. She supported numerous charities and often used her celebrity status to raise awareness and funds for causes close to her heart. During World War II, she actively participated in war bond drives, tirelessly traveling across the country to entertain and inspire troops. Her dedication to the cause earned her an honorary commission as a Colonel in the U.S. Army, a distinction she wore with pride.

In addition to her wartime efforts, Crawford advocated for children's causes and organizations that assisted the underprivileged. She became involved with the United Services Organization (USO) and the American Red Cross, organizing fundraisers and visiting hospitals and orphanages. Crawford's philanthropy extended internationally as well, as she lent her support to several international relief and aid organizations, such as UNICEF. Her compassion and dedication to helping those in need left a lasting impact on the lives of many.

Beyond her philanthropic work, Crawford also ventured into business outside of the entertainment industry. She invested in real estate, acquiring properties in Los Angeles and New York, demonstrating her keen business acumen. Additionally, Crawford successfully launched her own line of cosmetics in collaboration with a leading beauty brand, capitalizing on her image and reputation as a symbol of sophistication and beauty. Her cosmetics line became highly sought after and further solidified her position as an influential figure in both the entertainment and business worlds.

While Crawford's public image was carefully crafted to preserve and enhance her star status, her personal life revealed a woman who had triumphs, struggles, and a deep commitment to those she loved. Despite her glamorous persona, Crawford faced her fair share of challenges and setbacks, both in her personal life and career. However, her resilience and determination allowed her to navigate these obstacles with grace, ultimately solidifying her place in Hollywood history and leaving a legacy that extended far beyond the silver screen.

Chapter 15 delves into the lesser-known aspects of Joan Crawford's life outside of the spotlight, highlighting her personal relationships, philanthropy, and business endeavors. Through a deeper understanding of her life beyond the silver screen, readers gain insight into the complexities and nuances that shaped Crawford as a woman and as an icon.

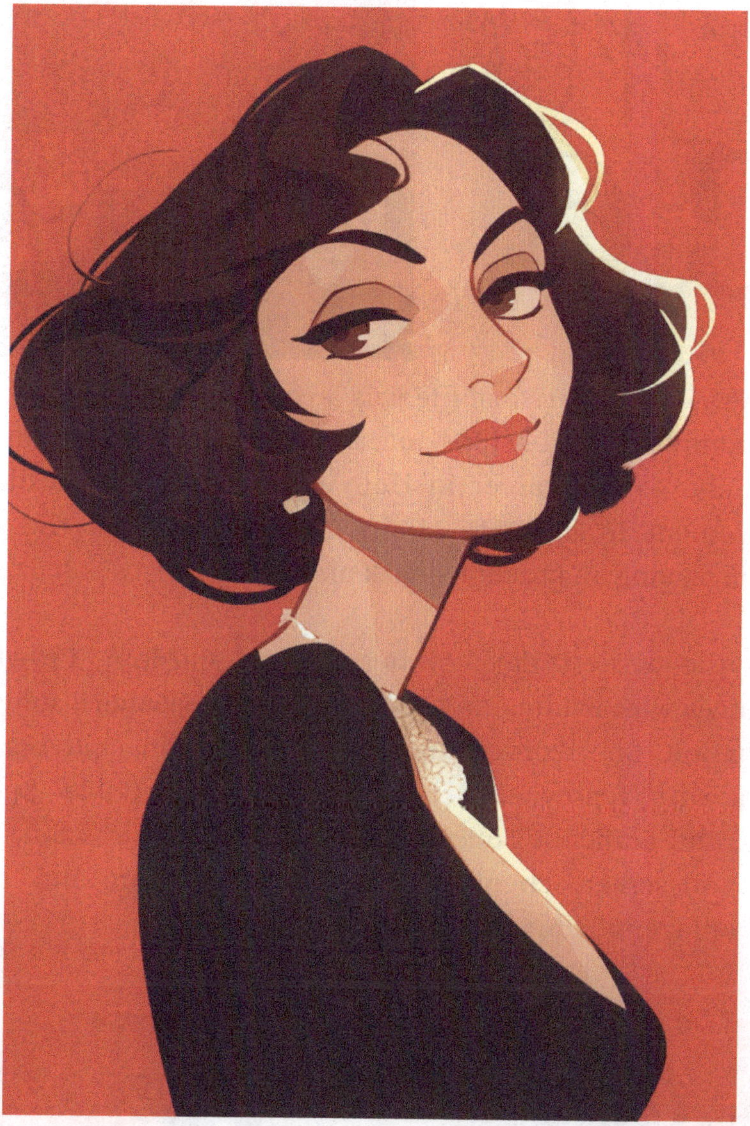

chapter 16

Personal relationships, marriages, and family

Joan Crawford's personal life was a captivating tapestry woven with complex relationships, marriages, and a deep commitment to family. As her career in Hollywood flourished, so did her involvement in intimate affairs that transcended the silver screen, leaving an indelible mark on her life.

From the earliest days of her rise to stardom, Crawford's romances with leading men in the industry became a subject of fascination. She exuded an aura of seduction, and her love affairs with renowned actors such as Clark Gable, Spencer Tracy, and Franchot Tone enthralled the media and fans alike. Their off-screen chemistry fueled speculation and added another layer of allure to Crawford's persona.

While her love affairs garnered attention, it was her marriages that defined significant chapters of her personal journey. Crawford, a woman whose life was often lived in the public eye, walked down the aisle four times, each marriage etching a distinct chapter in her history. Her first husband was actor Douglas Fairbanks Jr., and their marriage in 1929 marked a period of hope and ambition as they embarked on their journey as a glamorous couple in Hollywood. Together they symbolized the pinnacle of success and magnetism, but their fairytale crumbled as the pressures of fame and the strain of their individual careers took their toll. In 1933, their once-promising union concluded in a divorce that saddened both parties.

However, it was Crawford's marriage to actor Franchot Tone in 1935 that reignited the flames of romantic fervor in her life. Their relationship became the epitome of a passionate yet tumultuous love affair, punctuated by intense arguments followed by fervent reconciliations. Crawford, describing Tone as her "soulmate," had dreams of starting a family with him and engaging in a lifelong partnership. However, the pressures of their demanding careers and their deep-seated conflicting personal identities gradually eroded their connection. Their marriage, at times rocked by rumors of infidelity and alleged emotional abuse, reached a point of no return, and in 1939, they extinguished their vows in divorce. The public spectacle of their breakup, coated in scandalous whispers, left both individuals vulnerable to judgment and speculation.

Phillip Terry, an actor, entered Crawford's life as her third husband in 1942, bringing a renewed sense of stability and happiness. Their union was marked by a deep sense of camaraderie, and Crawford often referred to Terry as her source of strength and stability during those years. Together, they adopted two children, which further solidified Crawford's commitment to family. Sadly, as time passed, the harsh realities of their careers and their gradual emotional disconnect began corroding the bonds they had established. In 1946, they decided to untangle their intertwined lives through a divorce, but they remained on amicable terms, preserving a sense of respect and prioritizing the co-parenting of their children.

In 1955, Joan Crawford embarked on a new chapter of her personal life by marrying her fourth and final husband, Alfred Steele, the CEO of PepsiCo. Their marriage marked a transformative period for Crawford as she transitioned from the dazzling glamour of Hollywood to the boardrooms of the corporate world. Steele's position and wealth provided her with financial stability and a renewed sense of purpose. The marriage flourished, and Crawford became heavily involved in promoting PepsiCo, cementing her presence as a symbol of elegance and poise alongside the soda brand's iconic image. However, tragedy struck suddenly when Steele passed away from a heart attack in 1959, leaving Crawford shattered and bereaved.

While Crawford's marriages might have had their share of turbulence and challenges, her desire for companionship extended beyond the realm of romantic entanglements. She formed deep bonds with her four adopted children: Christina, Christopher, and the twins Cathy and Cindy. Crawford had always harbored a longing for a biological child, but fate had different plans. Driven by her love for children, she turned to adoption as a means of building her family. Crawford dedicated herself unconditionally to becoming the best mother she could be, offering the love and care she never experienced in her tumultuous childhood. Her devotion to her children became the anchor of her life.

However, the dynamic between Crawford and her eldest daughter, Christina, proved to be particularly tumultuous and contentious, providing more than its fair share of trials and tribulations. Christina's controversial memoir, "Mommie Dearest," portrayed Crawford as an abusive and controlling mother, and the book sparked heated debates and intense scrutiny. While some questioned the validity of Christina's accounts, many believed and empathized with her recollection of the emotional and physical abuse she endured. The revelations further intensified the public's fascination with Crawford's personal life, exploring the complexities of fame, love, and motherhood.

Despite the challenges and controversies that sometimes overshadowed her personal life, Joan Crawford's dedication to her children and advocacy for adoption remained steadfast. She utilized her platform and resources to create positive change, lending her voice and support to children's charities and adoption agencies. Through her philanthropic efforts, Crawford sought to uplift the often stigmatized perception of adoption and inspire others to embrace the power of love and family bonds.

Joan Crawford's personal life was a tapestry woven with passion, triumph, heartbreak, and resilience. Her relationships, marriages, and commitment to family added layers of depth to her public persona, shaping her legacy as both an actress and a woman of indomitable spirit. Her influence transcended the silver screen, leaving an enduring mark on the collective consciousness, and sparking ongoing conversations about the complexities of love, marriage, and the timeless significance of personal connections.

chatvariety.com

chapter 17

Philanthropy, business ventures, and off-screen pursuits

Throughout her illustrious career in Hollywood, Joan Crawford not only left an indelible mark on the silver screen but also used her success as a platform for philanthropy, entrepreneurship, and various off-screen pursuits.

Joan had a strong sense of social responsibility and a deep desire to give back to society. She knew that her celebrity status could be leveraged to make a positive impact, and she took this responsibility seriously. One cause that became particularly close to her heart was the fight against childhood cancer, as she had witnessed the devastating effects of the disease on her own family. Joan dedicated a significant amount of her time and efforts to raise awareness and funds for research, supporting organizations such as St. Jude Children's Research Hospital and the American Cancer Society. Her tireless advocacy and genuine compassion for young cancer patients garnered widespread respect and inspired others to join the cause.

Inspired by her own experiences as a young aspiring actress trying to break into the industry, Joan launched a foundation aimed at providing scholarships and financial assistance to aspiring artists. The Joan Crawford Foundation sought to empower those with artistic ambitions who might lack the resources to pursue their dreams fully. Through this foundation, Joan granted countless scholarships, mentoring programs, and financial aid to individuals studying various art forms, from acting and directing to writing and painting. Her support not only provided practical support but also motivated budding artists to continue pursuing their passions in the face of obstacles.

In addition to her philanthropic endeavors, Joan possessed a keen business acumen and a keen eye for opportunity. Recognizing the potential of her name and brand, she ventured into the world of fashion by launching her own line of clothing and accessories. The Joan Crawford Collection quickly gained popularity, attracting millions of fans who admired her glamorous style and sought to emulate her fashion choices. Joan's attention to detail, quality, and elegant designs set her collection apart, making it a staple for fashion-conscious individuals. But beyond her clothing line, Joan also collaborated with renowned designers and brands to create exclusive collections, ensuring that her influence extended beyond her own brand. Her business success not only reflected her impeccable taste but also provided her with a means to support her philanthropic endeavors further.

Not content with just one business venture, Joan also sought to share her experiences and wisdom through the written word. She authored several books, capturing both her personal journey and insights into her professional life. Her autobiography, "My Way of Life," became a bestseller, beloved by fans and aspiring actors alike. Joan's candid and honest account of her triumphs and struggles resonated with readers, inspiring them to pursue their dreams fearlessly. In addition to her autobiography, Joan wrote a series of self-help books, delving into topics such as personal growth, building resilience, and finding inner strength. These books became valuable resources for individuals seeking guidance and motivation in their own lives. Joan's entrepreneurial spirit and literary endeavors solidified her as not only an actress but also a multifaceted writer, mentor, and advocate.

Beyond her philanthropy and successful business ventures, Joan had a range of off-screen interests that mirrored her diverse skills and passions. She had an innate talent for art appreciation and became an avid collector. Joan carefully curated an extensive art collection, comprising pieces that reflected her discerning taste and appreciation for both modern and classical art. Her collection grew to include renowned works from artists such as Salvador Dali, Pablo Picasso, and Frida Kahlo. She graciously shared her collection with the public by organizing exhibitions and lending pieces to museums, allowing others to experience the beauty and power of art.

Joan's love for art extended to her own creative pursuits, as she developed her talent in painting and sculpture. She found solace in expressing herself through these mediums, creating captivating pieces that showcased her artistic flair and emotional depth. Joan's artwork captured the attention of art enthusiasts and critics, who were mesmerized by her ability to translate her complex emotions onto the canvas. Joan's works were displayed in exclusive galleries, with some pieces even sold to collectors who admired her unique vision and creativity.

Joan's off-screen pursuits did not end there. She also had a passion for interior design and home decor. Her exquisite taste was showcased in her meticulously curated homes, which were adorned with sophisticated furnishings, luxurious fabrics, and eclectic artwork. Each room reflected her personality and impeccable style, creating spaces that exuded elegance and allure. Joan's interior design skills earned her praise and admiration not only from the public but also from her peers in the industry. In fact, she even collaborated with renowned designers to create furniture pieces and home decor items that reflected her unique aesthetic.

Joan's dedication to philanthropy, business ventures, and off-screen pursuits showcased her multifaceted talent and unwavering commitment to making a difference in the world. Her ability to use her celebrity status to raise awareness and support causes close to her heart, her successful business ventures and entrepreneurial spirit, as well as her diverse artistic pursuits, solidified her status as not only an actress but also a true humanitarian, entrepreneur, writer, artist, and tastemaker whose influence extended far beyond the screen.

chatvariety.com

CHALLENGES AND RESILIENCE

chapter 18

Professional setbacks and comebacks

In the world of show business, setbacks are all too common, even for the most talented and successful individuals. Joan Crawford was no exception to this rule, as she experienced her fair share of professional highs and lows throughout her career. However, it was her remarkable ability to not only weather these setbacks but also bounce back stronger, that truly defined her as a resilient and enduring figure in Hollywood.

One of the most notable professional setbacks Crawford faced was the decline in her popularity and the diminishing quality of roles she was offered in the late 1940s and early 1950s. As the post-war era brought about changes in audience tastes and a shift in Hollywood's focus, Crawford found herself struggling to find projects that matched the success she had enjoyed in the previous decades. The rise of method acting and the emergence of newer stars posed a challenge to Crawford's more glamorous and traditional style of acting, causing her career to lose steam.

This period of professional stagnation was further compounded by personal turmoil. Following her highly publicized divorce from Franchot Tone, Crawford's personal life became tabloid fodder, affecting her public image. Additionally, her departure from Metro-Goldwyn-Mayer (MGM), the studio that had launched her career and where she thrived for years, resulted in a lack of prominent roles. Without the support of a major studio, Crawford had to fight to prove her relevance in a changing industry.

However, like a phoenix rising from the ashes, Crawford engineered a remarkable comeback in the mid-1950s. She made a bold decision to reinvent herself and take on challenging roles that showcased her versatility as an actress. It was during this time that she ventured into television, which provided a new avenue to showcase her talents.

One of the most significant turning points in her career was her collaboration with director Robert Aldrich in the film "Whatever Happened to Baby Jane?" (1962), where she starred alongside her longtime rival, Bette Davis. This unexpected pairing and Crawford's commanding performance in the role of Blanche Hudson marked a resurgence in her career. Despite the tension between the two actresses, their on-screen chemistry and powerful performances captivated audiences and generated considerable buzz.

The success of "Whatever Happened to Baby Jane?" helped Crawford shed her previous image and embrace edgier, more complex characters. She delved into psychological thrillers like "Strait-Jacket" (1964) and "Berserk!" (1967), playing women on the brink of insanity with a remarkable intensity. These roles showcased her ability to captivate audiences and reminded both critics and industry insiders of her immense talent, proving that she was more than just a former star attempting a comeback.

What set Crawford apart from others facing professional setbacks was not just her ability to reinvent herself, but also her unwavering determination and work ethic. She understood that success in Hollywood was not solely dependent on talent, but also on perseverance and the willingness to adapt. Crawford tirelessly prepared for her roles, immersing herself in research and investing time and effort into creating nuanced and compelling performances. Her relentless drive and commitment to her craft allowed her to overcome obstacles and prove that she was not just a fading star from the past but a force to be reckoned with in the present.

Crawford's comeback in her later years solidified her status as a Hollywood legend and secured her a place in the pantheon of great actresses. She continued to work tirelessly, taking on challenging roles in films like "The Damned Don't Cry" (1950), "Torch Song" (1953), and "What Ever Happened to Aunt Alice?" (1969). Her dedication to her craft even at an age when many actresses had retired was a testament to her love for acting and her enduring passion for her craft.

Moreover, Crawford's resilience extended beyond the world of acting. She faced constant scrutiny from the media and battled personal demons throughout her life, including struggles with alcoholism and difficult relationships. Yet, through it all, she managed to maintain her professionalism and dedication to her craft. Her ability to bounce back from setbacks in her personal and professional life, while not always evident to the public eye, showcases her true strength of character.

In conclusion, Joan Crawford's career was not without its share of professional setbacks, but it was her remarkable comebacks that truly shaped her legacy. Her ability to reinvent herself and take on challenging roles showcased her versatility as an actress, firmly establishing her as an enduring figure in Hollywood. Through her unwavering determination, meticulous preparation, and relentless work ethic, Crawford demonstrated that setbacks can be overcome, and success can be attained even in the face of adversity. Her story serves as a testament to the power of resilience and the indomitable spirit of those who refuse to be defined by their failures.

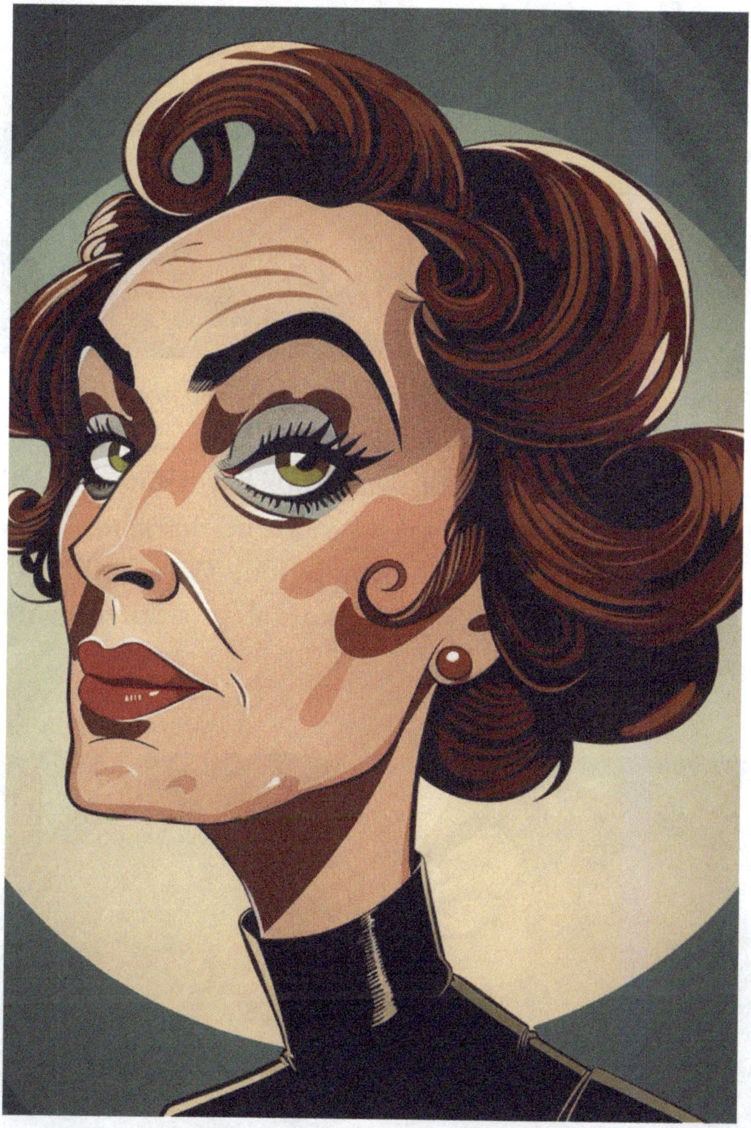

chapter 19

Personal trials and how she overcame them

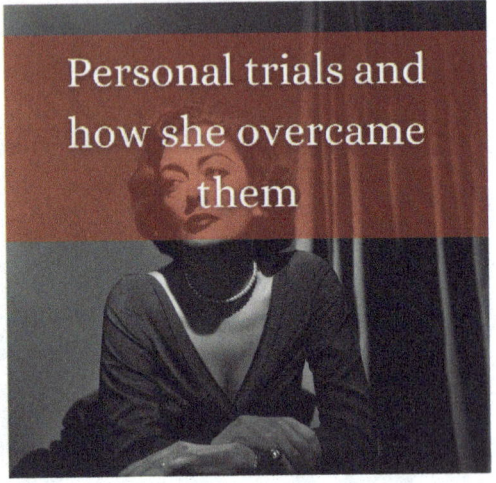

Joan Crawford's illustrious career was not without its fair share of personal trials and challenges. Behind the glamorous facade of Hollywood fame, she faced numerous hardships and setbacks that tested her resilience and strength of character. However, true to her unwavering determination, Crawford navigated these personal storms with remarkable resolve, emerging stronger than ever.

One of the most prominent personal trials Joan Crawford faced was her tumultuous relationships, specifically her four marriages. From her first husband, Douglas Fairbanks Jr., to her final union with Alfred Steele, the CEO of PepsiCo, Crawford's marriages were filled with both passion and heartbreak, offering a window into the complexities of her personal life. Each relationship proved to be a reflection of Crawford's own complicated and complex nature, as she relentlessly pursued love and happiness. Fueled by a desire for companionship, she sought solace in these marriages, only to find herself confronted with turmoil and disappointment. Despite facing numerous personal conflicts and failed relationships, she refused to be defined by her marital struggles. Crawford always managed to bounce back, picking up the pieces of her personal life and moving forward, determined to find love and happiness.

Growing up in poverty, Crawford's journey to Hollywood stardom was not an easy one, and her personal trials were a testament to her determination. Throughout her life, she faced deep-rooted insecurities and a constant fear of slipping back into poverty. This fear fueled her relentless work ethic, driving her to strive for success against all odds. The early years of her career were marked by grueling auditions, rejections, and financial hardships. Crawford's humble beginnings provided her with a relentless drive to succeed, as she knew firsthand the pain of struggle and the value of hard work. Her unwavering determination allowed her to persevere through these personal struggles, ultimately rising to become one of the most iconic actresses of the silver screen.

Further adding to the personal trials she endured was the strain of being a working mother in a time when it was not the societal norm. Crawford adopted her two children, Christina and Christopher, and sought to provide them with a stable and loving environment. Balancing her demanding career with the responsibilities of motherhood came with its own set of challenges. In an era where the concept of a single working mother was rare, she faced criticism and judgment from society. Yet, Crawford managed to create a strong bond with her children and was fiercely protective of their well-being, consistently putting their needs before her own. She worked tirelessly to ensure their happiness and success, reinforcing the idea that love and dedication can triumph over societal expectations and negative perceptions.

Another significant personal trial that Crawford faced was her battle with alcoholism. As pressure mounted in her career and personal life, Crawford turned to alcohol as a coping mechanism, seeking solace in its numbing effects. However, she soon realized the destructive path she was on and made the brave decision to seek treatment for her addiction. In her quest for recovery, Crawford embarked on a personal journey of self-discovery, delving into the root causes of her reliance on alcohol. Through therapy, introspection, and a strong support network, she successfully overcame her struggles with alcoholism, further solidifying her status as a resilient and determined woman. Her triumph over addiction stands as a testament to her unwavering willpower and serves as an inspiration for others facing similar challenges.

In addition to these personal trials, Crawford also faced professional setbacks throughout her career. As the industry evolved and she aged, she experienced a decline in the number of high-profile roles being offered to her. Undeterred, she never ceased in her efforts to remain relevant. Crawford reinvented herself time and again, taking on new challenges and proving her versatility as an actress. She delved into television and stage performances, showcasing her talent across different mediums. Her resilience and ability to adapt ensured her longevity in the industry, as she continued to leave her mark on the entertainment world. Despite the changing tides of the industry, Crawford's enduring legacy remains a testament to her ability to overcome professional setbacks and redefine her career on her own terms.

Joan Crawford's ability to overcome and rise above personal trials serves as an inspiration to all. Throughout her life, she demonstrated strength, resilience, and an unwavering commitment to her craft. Her journey from rags to riches, coupled with her personal triumphs, showcased the transformative power of perseverance and determination. She weathered the storms of personal relationships, battled her own demons, and faced professional obstacles head-on, emerging victorious each time. In the face of adversity, Crawford never shied away from confronting her personal trials, allowing her to emerge not only as a Hollywood legend but also as a symbol of strength and resilience. Her life serves as a timeless inspiration for generations to come, reminding us that strength can be found within ourselves even in the darkest of times.

chatvariety.com

chapter 20

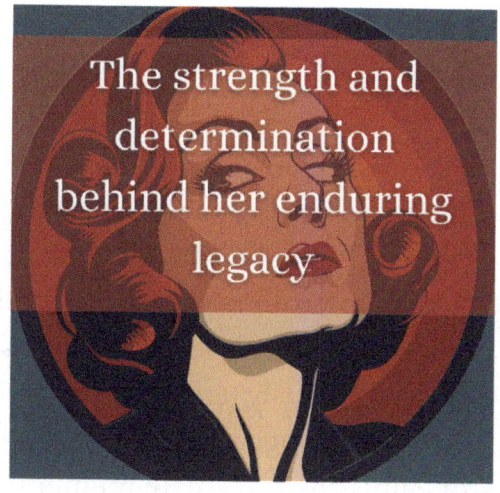

The strength and determination behind her enduring legacy

Joan Crawford's enduring legacy in Hollywood is not only attributed to her immense talent and on-screen presence but also to her strength and determination in the face of numerous challenges throughout her life and career.

One of Crawford's remarkable qualities was her unwavering determination to succeed. From her early days as a struggling actress to her rise to fame, she consistently displayed a tenacity that propelled her forward. Born Lucille Fay LeSueur, she had a difficult childhood, marked by poverty and instability. Her parents divorced when she was young, and her mother remarried several times, exposing her to various hardships and uncertainty. However, even in the face of adversity, she dreamed of a better life and had an unwavering belief in her own abilities.

Crawford relentlessly pursued her passion for acting, sacrificing comfort and security for the pursuit of her dreams. She knew that success was not handed to her on a silver platter but had to be earned through hard work and perseverance. Starting from humble beginnings as a chorus girl, she honed her craft and gradually climbed the ladder of success. Crawford's determination to succeed was evident in her tireless efforts to improve her acting skills and enhance her on-screen presence. She meticulously studied every aspect of her performances, from her dialogue delivery to her body language, leaving no stone unturned to create memorable characters that captivated audiences.

Her strength was not just limited to her professional life. In her personal life, she faced many hardships as well. Her early marriages were tumultuous, marked by abuse and infidelity. Despite the toxic relationships she endured, she never lost sight of her own worth. She made the difficult decision to leave those harmful situations behind, showing immense courage and resilience. Crawford's ability to break free from such damaging circumstances and rebuild her life is a testament to her indomitable spirit.

Tragedy struck Crawford's life when she experienced the heartbreak of losing her adopted daughter Christina to cancer. The loss of a child is a profound pain that can shatter even the strongest individuals. Yet, Crawford found the strength to continue on, channeling her grief into her work and using her platform to raise awareness and funds for cancer research. Her ability to transform personal pain into a force for good is a testament to her remarkable character and the depth of her compassion.

Behind the scenes, Crawford was known for her tireless work ethic. She was famous for her meticulous preparation and dedication to her craft. She understood that true success is not achieved without hard work and perseverance. Despite her glamorous image, she never shied away from getting her hands dirty, often involving herself in the minutiae of filmmaking to ensure every detail was perfect. She believed in relentless self-improvement and was not afraid to put in the necessary time and effort to perfect her performances. This dedication allowed her to consistently deliver exceptional work and solidify her place as one of Hollywood's finest actresses.

Crawford's determination was also evident in her willingness to take risks and embrace new challenges. As she aged, she faced the inevitable changes in the film industry. Many actors struggle to find relevant roles as they grow older, but not Crawford. Instead of allowing herself to be sidelined, she took on unconventional roles and ventured into television. With each new project, she proved her versatility and adaptability, defying expectations and reinventing herself time and time again. Her ability to adapt to the changing times is a testament to her forward-thinking nature and her refusal to be limited by age or societal expectations.

Furthermore, Crawford's strength and determination extended beyond her career. She had a deep sense of compassion and a keen understanding of the power she held as a public figure. Throughout her life, she used her influence to champion important causes. During World War II, she tirelessly supported the troops, tirelessly touring military installations and entertaining soldiers. She understood the significance of her role in lifting spirits and boosting morale during such challenging times.

Crawford also fervently advocated for the rights of children. Drawing from her own experiences growing up in an unstable environment, she championed organizations such as the United Service Organizations and the National Playground Association. She believed in providing a safe and nurturing environment for children, and she used her fame to raise awareness and funds for these causes. Crawford's dedication to making a difference in the lives of others showcased her incredible compassion and commitment to leaving a lasting impact beyond the silver screen.

Joan Crawford's enduring legacy rests upon her remarkable ability to overcome adversity, her relentless pursuit of excellence, and her unwavering strength and determination. Her story is a testament to the human spirit's ability to rise above challenges and achieve greatness. Crawford's legacy serves as an inspiration to generations of actors and artists, reminding them that success is not merely a result of talent but of resilience, fortitude, and never giving up on one's dreams.

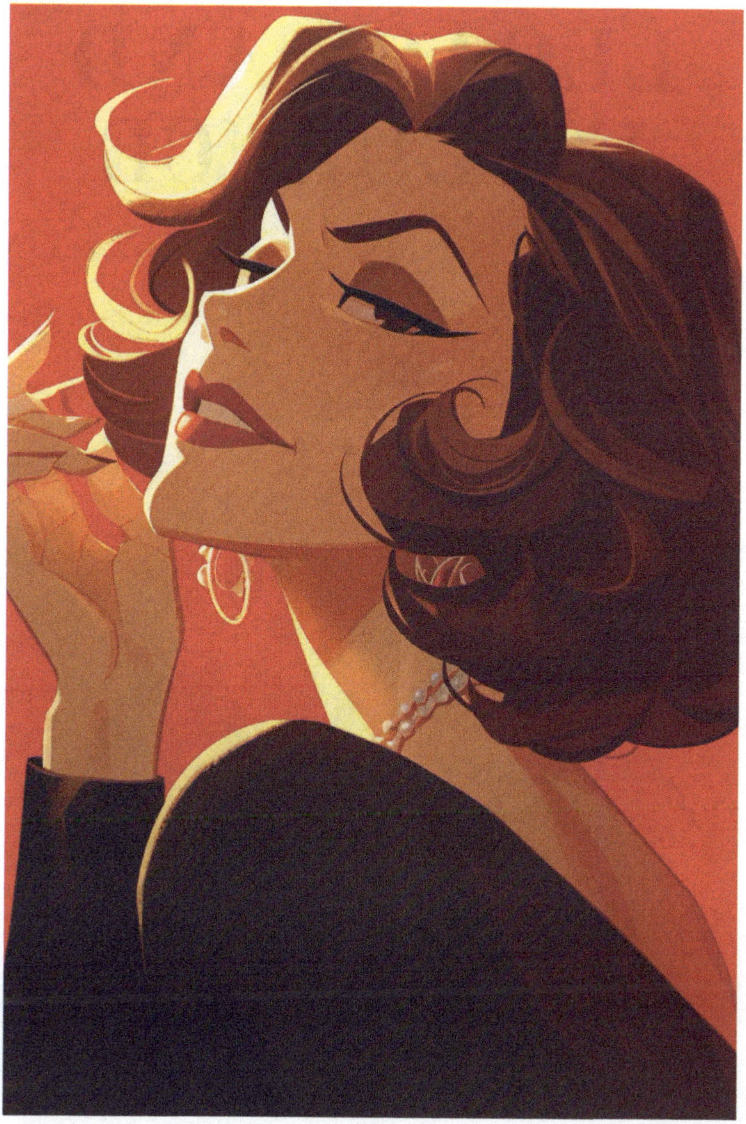

LEGACY AND INFLUENCE

chapter 21

Reflection on her impact on future generations of actors and filmmakers

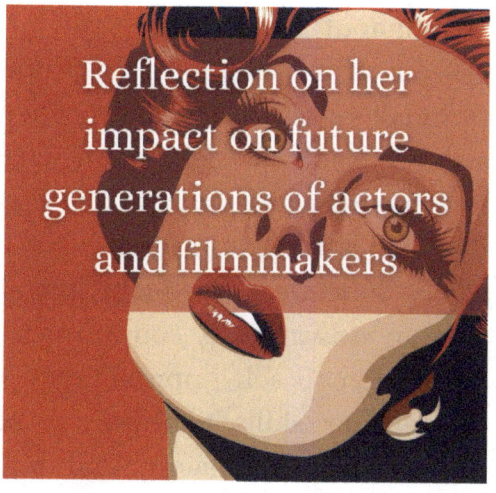

Throughout her illustrious and transformative career, Joan Crawford left an indelible mark on the entertainment industry. Her incomparable talent, unwavering determination, and relentless commitment to her craft continue to shape and inspire future generations of actors and filmmakers, elevating the art of storytelling and influencing the course of Hollywood history.

One of the most significant aspects of Crawford's impact was her unwavering determination to break free from the limitations and stereotypes placed on women in the film industry of her time. In an era where women were often relegated to secondary roles or portrayed in one-dimensional stereotypes, Crawford defied expectations and challenged societal norms. With her iconic performances that pushed boundaries, she shattered glass ceilings and paved the way for future actresses to embrace multidimensional roles, explore complex characters, and command the spotlight. Her influential work extended far beyond the screen, inspiring women in all fields to recognize their worth, embrace their individuality, and fearlessly pursue their dreams despite societal expectations.

Throughout her career, Crawford's unparalleled work ethic served as a beacon of inspiration for aspiring actors and filmmakers alike. She approached each role with a relentless ardor, constantly seeking new challenges and refusing to settle for mediocrity. Crawford's tireless pursuit of excellence demonstrated that success in the entertainment industry is not solely dependent on talent but also on hard work, discipline, and an unwavering commitment to honing one's craft. Her dedication to self-improvement and her relentless hunger to master her skills continue to serve as a testament to the importance of tenacity and a growth mindset within the creative realm.

Beyond her determination, Crawford's monumental impact can be seen in her adaptability and resilience. Her career spanned nearly five decades, a remarkable feat that exemplifies her ability to evolve with the times and remain relevant in an ever-changing industry. Throughout different eras, Crawford fearlessly reinvented herself, demonstrating that artistic longevity arises from the willingness to embrace change and adapt to the transforming landscape of the entertainment industry. Her versatility and ability to seamlessly transition between genres and character archetypes influenced subsequent generations of actors and filmmakers, encouraging them to venture outside their comfort zones and explore new artistic horizons.

Moreover, Crawford's influence can be measured not only through her professional achievements but also in the personal connections she cultivated with younger actors. As an established Hollywood star, she often took aspiring talents under her wing, mentoring and nurturing their budding careers. Crawford's empathetic and generous nature allowed her to share her wealth of knowledge and experiences, providing invaluable guidance and encouragement to those who looked up to her. Her belief in the potential of future generations and her commitment to fostering their growth propelled them forward, carrying her legacy of excellence and compassion as they stepped into the spotlight and made their own mark on the industry.

In addition to the individual impact she had on actors and filmmakers, Crawford's indomitable spirit reshaped the wider film industry. Her innovative approach to acting and her willingness to take risks challenged conventions and pushed the boundaries of storytelling. Through her revolutionary performances, she introduced new storytelling techniques, such as method acting and psychological realism, to the cinematic landscape. Crawford's mastery of lighting, camera angles, and character psychology influenced filmmakers to explore uncharted territories, experiment with different visual and narrative styles, and create unforgettable cinematic experiences. Her artistic legacy can be seen in the evolution of motion picture techniques and the continued exploration of the human psyche on screen.

Furthermore, beyond her contributions as a trailblazer in acting, Crawford's impact radiated as a savvy businesswoman and entrepreneur. She navigated the complexities of the industry and seized opportunities to take control of her own destiny, becoming one of the first actors to secure creative control and ownership of her films. Crawford's business acumen and determination to carve her path empowered future actors and filmmakers to not only focus on their artistic endeavors but also assert their creative vision, challenge systemic powers, and shape the industry from within. Her legacy serves as a reminder that artistic brilliance and entrepreneurial spirit can coexist, empowering individuals to break free from industry constraints and drive transformative change.

In conclusion, Joan Crawford's impact on future generations of actors and filmmakers is immeasurable. Her fearlessness, determination, and artistic brilliance continue to reverberate throughout the entertainment industry, shaping the way stories are told and inspiring others to push through barriers and defy expectations. From breaking gender barriers to inspiring resilience, adaptability, and artistic exploration, Crawford's enduring influence demonstrates the transformative power of the performing arts. Her remarkable journey serves as a guiding light, reminding aspiring actors and filmmakers of the profound impact they can have on future generations, encouraging them to embrace their unique voices, and empowering them to leave an indelible legacy of their own.

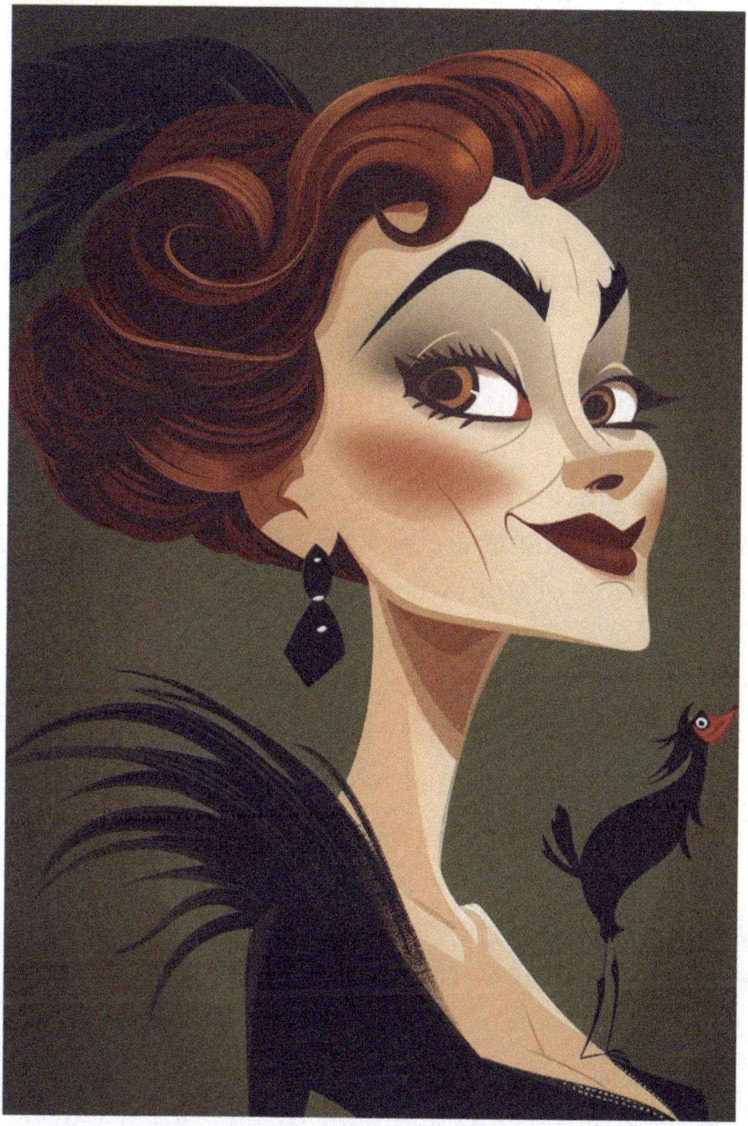

chapter 22

Joan Crawford's place in Hollywood history and popular culture

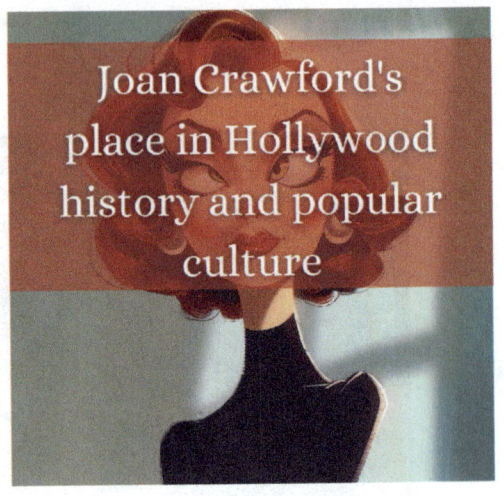

Joan Crawford's impact on Hollywood history and popular culture is indisputable. With a career that spanned several decades, she left an indelible mark on the silver screen and continues to be remembered and revered as one of the legends of the Golden Age of Hollywood.

Crawford's rise to stardom was not an easy one. Born Lucille Fay LeSueur in San Antonio, Texas, on March 23, 1905, she faced a challenging childhood marked by poverty and uncertainty. Raised by a single mother, Crawford witnessed her mother's struggles to provide for the family, often taking on odd jobs to make ends meet. This early exposure to hardship and adversity ingrained in Crawford a strong work ethic and determination to escape her circumstances.

Her first taste of the entertainment world came when she won a dance contest in Kansas City at the age of 16. It was during this contest that she caught the eye of a talent scout who was captivated by her natural grace and presence. Recognizing her potential, the scout persuaded Crawford to consider a career in show business.

In 1925, Crawford arrived in Los Angeles, ready to pursue her dreams. She began working as a chorus girl in various productions before catching the attention of MGM studio head, Louis B. Mayer. Mayer signed Crawford to a contract and decided to change her name from Lucille Fay LeSueur to the more marketable "Joan Crawford."

With her devotion to perfecting her acting craft, Crawford quickly established herself as a leading lady. Her breakthrough came in 1928 with the film "Our Dancing Daughters," directed by Harry Beaumont. In this silent film, Crawford portrayed a liberated flapper girl named Diana Medford, depicting the spirit of the Roaring Twenties. The film became a box office success, grossing over $1.5 million, which was an astonishing amount for that time. Crawford's portrayal resonated with audiences, particularly young women who were embracing newfound independence, and catapulted her to fame.

Throughout her career, Crawford exhibited unparalleled versatility as an actress. From melodrama to film noir, she effortlessly transitioned between genres and captivated audiences with her intensity and emotional depth. While she initially mastered the world of silent film, Crawford made a seamless transition to talkies in 1929, proving that her talent extended beyond silent visual storytelling. She showcased her range in films such as "Grand Hotel" (1932), where she starred alongside Greta Garbo and John Barrymore, and "The Women" (1939), a witty and biting satire on female relationships.

One of Crawford's most acclaimed performances came in the 1945 film "Mildred Pierce," directed by Michael Curtiz. In this noir-inspired melodrama, she played the title character, a self-sacrificing mother who becomes a successful businesswoman to provide for her ungrateful daughter. This role not only earned her an Academy Award for Best Actress but also solidified her reputation as one of the industry's most talented and dedicated actresses. Despite facing stiff competition from actresses like Ingrid Bergman and Greer Garson, Crawford's remarkable performance in "Mildred Pierce" propelled her to the top and cemented her status as a Hollywood icon.

Crawford's personal life was often tumultuous, with a string of marriages and high-profile relationships. Her marriages to Douglas Fairbanks Jr., Franchot Tone, and Philip Terry captured the attention of the press and fueled public fascination with her personal affairs. Her marriage to actor Franchot Tone, particularly, caused a frenzy as their on-screen chemistry in films such as "The Bride Wore Red" (1937) seemed to mirror their real-life relationship. Despite multiple marriages ending in divorce, Crawford's determination to juggle her personal life and professional career remained unwavering.

In the later years of her career, Crawford experienced a revival through her collaboration with director Robert Aldrich on the cult classic "Whatever Happened to Baby Jane?" (1962). In this psychological thriller, she co-starred alongside her long-time rival Bette Davis, creating a dynamic and riveting on-screen presence. The film marked a departure from her glamorous star image, as Crawford portrayed an aging former child star trapped in a decrepit mansion. With her performance as Blanche Hudson, Crawford showcased her ability to embrace complex and edgy roles, further solidifying her reputation as a versatile actress capable of tackling unconventional characters.

Beyond her acting career, Crawford's activism and philanthropy were integral parts of her legacy. She actively supported the war effort during World War II, participating in the Hollywood Canteen and entertaining troops. Her dedication to charitable causes extended to her involvement with various organizations, including the American Cancer Society and the March of Dimes. Crawford's commitment to giving back truly exemplified her compassionate nature and desire to make a positive impact beyond the silver screen.

In addition to her philanthropy, Crawford's business ventures showcased her astute business acumen. In the early 1950s, she embarked on a partnership with the PepsiCo corporation, which led her to become one of the first women on the board of directors for a major corporation. Crawford's involvement with PepsiCo, along with her charismatic presence in advertising campaigns, significantly bolstered the company's image and marketing strategies, expanding its reach and making significant contributions to its success.

Today, Joan Crawford's influence can still be felt throughout Hollywood and popular culture. Her films continue to be celebrated, studied, and referenced by filmmakers, actors, and film enthusiasts alike. Her timeless beauty and unforgettable performances inspire actors of all generations. Film historians and scholars analyze her work, delving into the complexities of her persona and the impact she had on the industry as a woman in a time dominated by men.

Joan Crawford's place in Hollywood history and popular culture is firmly secured as a trailblazer, an icon, and a symbol of resilience. From her humble beginnings to her extraordinary rise to stardom, Crawford will forever be remembered as a true Hollywood legend—a remarkable actress, a businesswoman, and a woman who defied expectations and left an indelible imprint on the world of entertainment.

chatvariety.com

chapter 23

Tributes and memorials celebrating her life and career

Throughout Joan Crawford's illustrious career, she captivated audiences with her stunning performances, leaving an indelible mark on the world of cinema. Following her passing in 1977, fans and industry colleagues alike came together to pay tribute to the legendary actress and honor her extraordinary contributions to the entertainment industry.

In the wake of her death, tributes poured in from all corners of the globe, as admirers shared their fondest memories and celebrated the impact Crawford had on their lives. Fans organized gatherings and memorial services, where they discussed her iconic performances, shared anecdotes, and expressed their gratitude for her talent and charisma.

One remarkable tribute to Crawford's legacy was the establishment of The Joan Crawford Memorial Foundation, dedicated to preserving and promoting her contributions to film, fashion, and philanthropy. The foundation, initially established by a group of devoted fans, quickly gained support from friends, family, and industry professionals who recognized the importance of preserving her memory. Through donations and fundraising efforts, the foundation was able to create a variety of programs and initiatives that celebrated her life and career.

The foundation's efforts included the preservation and restoration of Crawford's films, ensuring that future generations could continue to appreciate her artistry. It also funded scholarships and mentorship programs for aspiring actors, recognizing Crawford's own struggles to establish herself in the industry and her commitment to supporting young talent. Additionally, the foundation organized exhibitions and retrospectives, showcasing Crawford's costumes, personal memorabilia, and behind-the-scenes photos, allowing fans and scholars to explore her life and creative process. These initiatives helped to keep her legacy alive and accessible to all those eager to delve into her remarkable career.

Hollywood itself paid tribute to Crawford's remarkable career by showcasing some of her most beloved films in special screenings and retrospectives. The Academy of Motion Picture Arts and Sciences hosted extensive retrospectives honoring Crawford's diverse body of work, showcasing her versatility and the sheer breadth of her talent. These events served as a reminder of her lasting influence on the art of cinema and provided an opportunity for both seasoned critics and new audiences to appreciate her craft.

Crawford's peers in the film industry also came together to honor her legacy. Fellow actors, directors, and producers spoke fondly of their experiences working with her and shared personal stories that showcased her dedication and professionalism. Many acknowledged her as a trailblazer for female actors, breaking barriers and paving the way for generations to come. In recognition of her contributions, the Screen Actors Guild not only established the "Joan Crawford Award for Excellence," honoring outstanding performances by actresses who embody Crawford's spirit and determination but also created the Joan Crawford Fund for Emerging Artists. This fund supported promising actors, writers, and directors at the early stages of their careers, providing them with crucial financial aid and mentorship opportunities.

In addition to public tributes, Crawford's memory lives on through various memorials and monuments dedicated to her life and career. Several institutions and organizations have erected statues, plaques, and other commemorative displays in her honor. These physical tributes serve as a permanent reminder of her immense contributions and continue to inspire new generations of artists and fans. The Joan Crawford Memorial Garden, located in her hometown of San Antonio, features a grand statue of the actress surrounded by lush flowers and trees, serving as a serene space where fans can reflect on her enduring legacy and pay their respects.

Moreover, the impact of Joan Crawford's career can be seen in the ongoing influence she has on popular culture. Her iconic fashion sense, signature roles, and fierce determination have become enduring symbols of strength and resilience. Countless books, documentaries, and biopics have been created to explore and celebrate her life story, further cementing her status as a cultural icon. For example, the critically acclaimed documentary "Joan Crawford: The Legacy Continues" not only delves into her life beyond the glamour but also explores her complex relationships, her tireless work ethic, and her struggles with the rigid Hollywood system. By shedding light on the less-known aspects of Crawford's life, this documentary encourages audiences to appreciate the depth and complexity of her legacy.

Furthermore, the legacy of Joan Crawford extends beyond the world of film. Her philanthropic efforts and activism in various causes continue to inspire and make a difference in the lives of many. From supporting children's charities to advocating for women's rights, Crawford's impact reaches far beyond the silver screen. The Joan Crawford Foundation for Children, established in her honor, continues to fund educational programs, health initiatives, and arts scholarships, embodying Crawford's dedication to helping others. The foundation has expanded its reach globally, working in collaboration with other organizations to bring positive change to communities around the world. Through partnerships with schools, hospitals, and non-profit organizations, the foundation's efforts have touched countless lives, carrying on Crawford's compassionate spirit in the modern world.

In conclusion, the tributes and memorials dedicated to Joan Crawford honor the extraordinary life and career of one of Hollywood's most enduring legends. Whether through public events, physical monuments, ongoing cultural references, or philanthropic initiatives, her influence remains as strong as ever. As fans continue to discover her films, explore her life story, and participate in the programs established in her name, Joan Crawford's legacy as a trailblazer and icon of the silver screen will continue to shine brightly, inspiring new generations of artists and audiences alike.

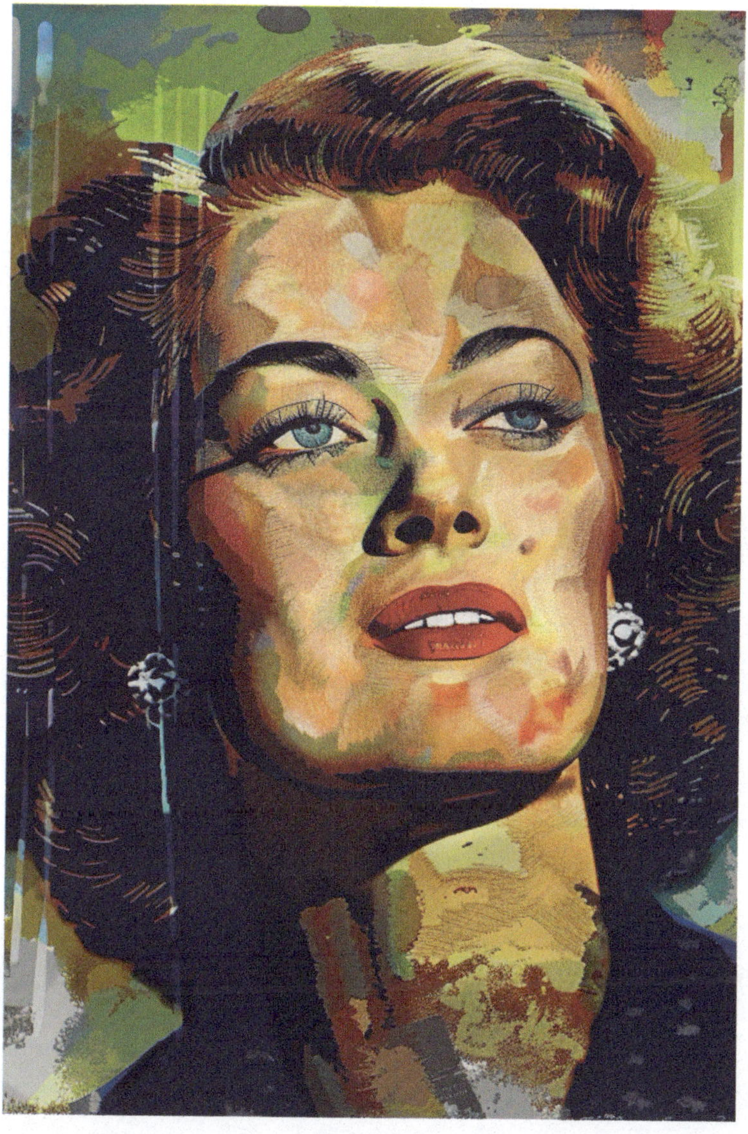

CONCLUSION

chapter 24

Summation of Joan Crawford's journey from rags to riches

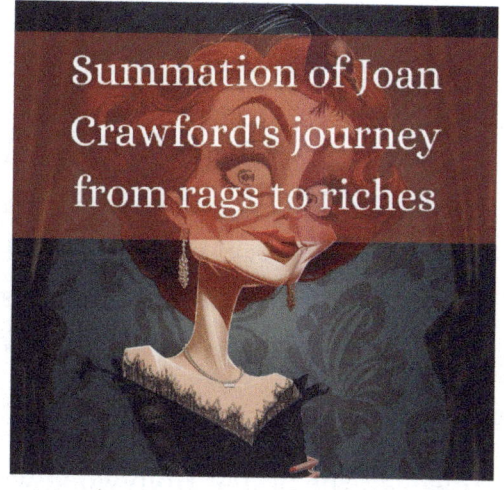

Joan Crawford's life is a true testament to the power of transformation and the relentless pursuit of success. From humble beginnings to becoming one of Hollywood's most iconic and enduring figures, her journey from rags to riches is an inspiring tale of passion, determination, and resilience. Decades after her passing, her legacy continues to inspire audiences around the world.

Born Lucille Fay LeSueur on March 23, 1904, in San Antonio, Texas, Joan faced numerous challenges right from the start. Her early years were marked by poverty and instability, as her father deserted the family shortly after her birth. Raised by her mother and stepfather, Joan witnessed firsthand the difficulties of making ends meet and the harsh realities of life. However, rather than succumbing to adversity, she forged ahead with unwavering determination and a fierce desire to rise above her circumstances.

Joan's natural talent for dance and performance emerged at a young age. With dreams of escaping her difficult life, she embarked on a journey in show business. She joined various dance troupes, touring the country and gaining invaluable experience and exposure. It was during this time that she fell in love with the world of theater and discovered her true passion for acting. The stage became her sanctuary, a place where she could fully express herself and captivate audiences with her talent.

However, the pull of Hollywood was irresistible, and Joan knew she needed to seize the opportunity if she wanted to fulfill her dreams. In her early twenties, she took a leap of faith and moved to Los Angeles. Armed with determination and a burning desire to succeed, she dove headfirst into auditions and tirelessly pursued opportunities to showcase her abilities.

It was in 1925, after a series of auditions and setbacks, that Joan caught the attention of MGM studios. They recognized her magnetic screen presence and signed her to a contract, marking the beginning of her ascent to stardom. Under the guidance of the studio, Joan honed her craft, refining her skills and navigating the intricate world of Hollywood with grace and determination.

Joan's career flourished throughout the 1930s and 1940s. Films like "Grand Hotel," "Mildred Pierce," "Possessed," and "Whatever Happened to Baby Jane?" showcased her versatility as an actress and solidified her status as a Hollywood legend. With her striking beauty, piercing eyes, and emotional intensity, she had the ability to fully inhabit her characters, leaving audiences mesmerized.

Beyond her on-screen success, Joan's personal life was a constant topic of fascination. She married four times, each marriage accompanied by its share of controversy and turmoil. Her tumultuous relationship with fellow actor and husband, Franchot Tone, captivated the public's attention, contributing to her image as a woman with a complex and intriguing private life.

However, as Joan gracefully aged, she faced the challenges of an industry that often dismissed and marginalized older actresses. Determined to prove her worth, she reinvented herself through embracing the horror genre. Her collaboration with director Robert Aldrich in "What Ever Happened to Baby Jane?" marked a pivotal moment in her career, showcasing her ability to embrace darkness and redefine her image. The film's success breathed new life into her career, catapulting her into a new phase of fame and demonstrating that talent knows no expiration date.

Throughout her journey, Joan Crawford's fiery spirit and relentless pursuit of greatness were evident. She refused to let societal expectations or the limitations of her age define her. Joan's resilience and unyielding commitment to her craft opened doors for women in the industry, becoming a symbol of empowerment and breaking the glass ceiling. She fearlessly challenged norms, proving that a woman's worth and talent transcended society's preconceived notions.

Today, Joan Crawford's legacy remains indelible and vibrant. Her name evokes images of strength, determination, and glamour. Her story teaches us that no matter where we come from or what challenges we face, we have the power to shape our destiny and overcome adversity.

Joan Crawford's impact extends beyond her films. Her dedication to her craft, her commitment to excellence, and her unwavering spirit continue to inspire countless actors and artists. Through her artistry and resilience, she became a trailblazer and an inspiration for generations to come.

In contemplating Joan Crawford's journey from rags to riches, her story delves deep into the human spirit's ability to rise above circumstances and embrace one's true potential. Her remarkable transformation and unyielding determination serve as a guiding light, fueling the flames of hope and ambition within those yearning for transformation. Joan Crawford's legacy continues to illuminate paths to greatness, encouraging us all to seize life's opportunities, believe in ourselves, and create our own destinies.

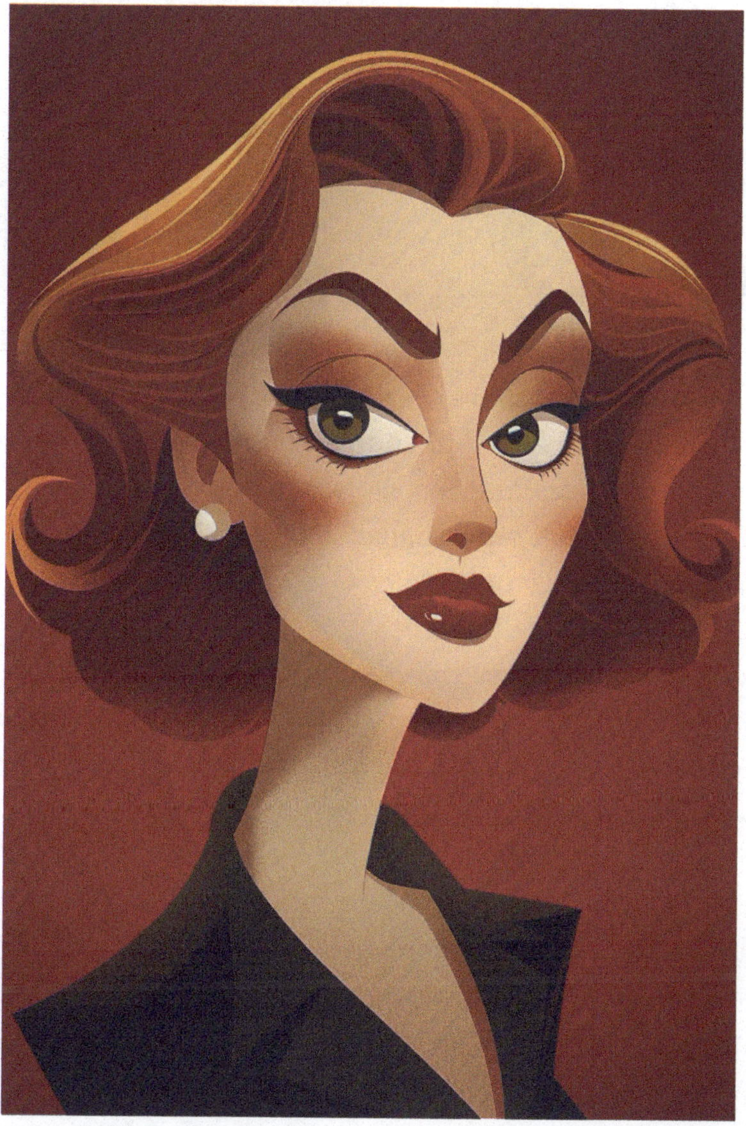

chapter 25

The enduring qualities that define her legacy

Throughout her illustrious career and beyond, Joan Crawford's legacy is defined by several enduring qualities that continue to captivate audiences and inspire aspiring actors and actresses. These qualities not only shaped her as a performer but also made her a cultural icon.

One of the key qualities that defined Joan Crawford's legacy is her indomitable determination. From her humble beginnings in San Antonio, Texas, to her rise as a Hollywood star, Crawford displayed an unwavering commitment to her craft that was imprinted in her very being. Raised by a single mother, Crawford knew early on that success would not come easily, and she was prepared to work tirelessly to achieve her dreams. She refused to let any obstacle stand in her way and was relentlessly dedicated to honing her skills and delivering memorable performances. Throughout her career, she underwent rigorous training to improve her acting, voice, and dancing abilities, constantly pushing herself to surpass her own limitations. This determination not only propelled her to the top of the industry but also earned her the respect and admiration of her peers.

Another defining quality of Joan Crawford's legacy is her immense versatility as an actress. Throughout her career, she showcased her ability to effortlessly transition between different genres and roles, proving her range time and time again. She was equally adept at playing seductive femme fatales in film noir classics like "Mildred Pierce" as she was at embodying romantic heroines in sweeping melodramas like "Humoresque." Crawford brought a depth and authenticity to every character she played, delving deep into their emotions and motivations. Her ability to transform herself completely into each role allowed audiences to connect with her characters on a profound level and made her performances stand the test of time. Whether she was portraying a conniving social climber or a self-sacrificing mother, Crawford's captivating presence and nuanced portrayals captivated the hearts of audiences worldwide. Her versatility allowed her to remain relevant and sought after in an ever-changing film landscape, cementing her status as one of the greatest actresses of her time.

Crawford's enduring legacy is also deeply influenced by her resilience, both onscreen and off. Throughout her life, she faced numerous personal and professional challenges, and she consistently bounced back and reinvented herself time and time again. From navigating the transition from silent films to talkies, where many actors struggled to adapt, to dealing with the pressures of aging in Hollywood, Crawford demonstrated an indomitable spirit that allowed her to overcome adversity. She embraced change and was not afraid to take risks, continually pushing herself to evolve as an artist. Despite personal setbacks and tragedies, including failed marriages and the loss of loved ones, Crawford demonstrated a remarkable resilience that allowed her to rise above her circumstances. Her ability to endure and triumph over adversity was a testament to her inner strength and unwavering determination.

Additionally, Joan Crawford's dedication to her craft and her work ethic also significantly contributed to her enduring legacy. Known for her meticulous preparation and attention to detail, she approached each role with a level of professionalism that set her apart from her peers. Crawford was known to immerse herself completely in her characters, spending hours studying scripts, rehearsing, and perfecting her performances. She left no stone unturned in her quest for authenticity, diligently researching the time period, dialects, and mannerisms of her characters. This commitment to her craft resulted in performances that were nuanced, layered, and deeply affecting. Crawford believed that there was no substitute for hard work and dedication, and she expected the same level of commitment from those she worked with. Her unwavering dedication and tireless work ethic inspired not only admiration but also a sense of awe among her peers.

Lastly, the impact that Joan Crawford made off-screen is an essential aspect of her enduring legacy that deserves recognition. Throughout her life, she participated in numerous charitable endeavors and actively supported various causes, including cancer research and the welfare of children. Crawford truly understood the power of her platform as a beloved actress and used her influence to bring attention to important social issues. Her generosity and compassion extended far beyond the realm of entertainment, reflecting her deep empathy for those in need. Crawford's philanthropic efforts were not just a means to enhance her public image; they were a genuine reflection of her belief in using her position of privilege to make a positive impact in the world. Her charitable work left a lasting impression, not only on the individuals and communities she helped but also on the collective conscience of society at large.

In conclusion, the enduring qualities that define Joan Crawford's legacy are her indomitable determination, immense versatility, unwavering resilience, unwavering dedication, and impactful philanthropy. These qualities not only made her an icon in the entertainment industry but also continue to inspire individuals to pursue their dreams, overcome obstacles, and make a positive impact in the world. Joan Crawford's enduring legacy serves as a testament to her talent, strength, and the indelible mark she left on Hollywood and beyond. Her determination, versatility, resilience, dedication to her craft, and her philanthropy continue to inspire and uplift generations to come, solidifying her place as one of the most influential and beloved figures in the history of film.

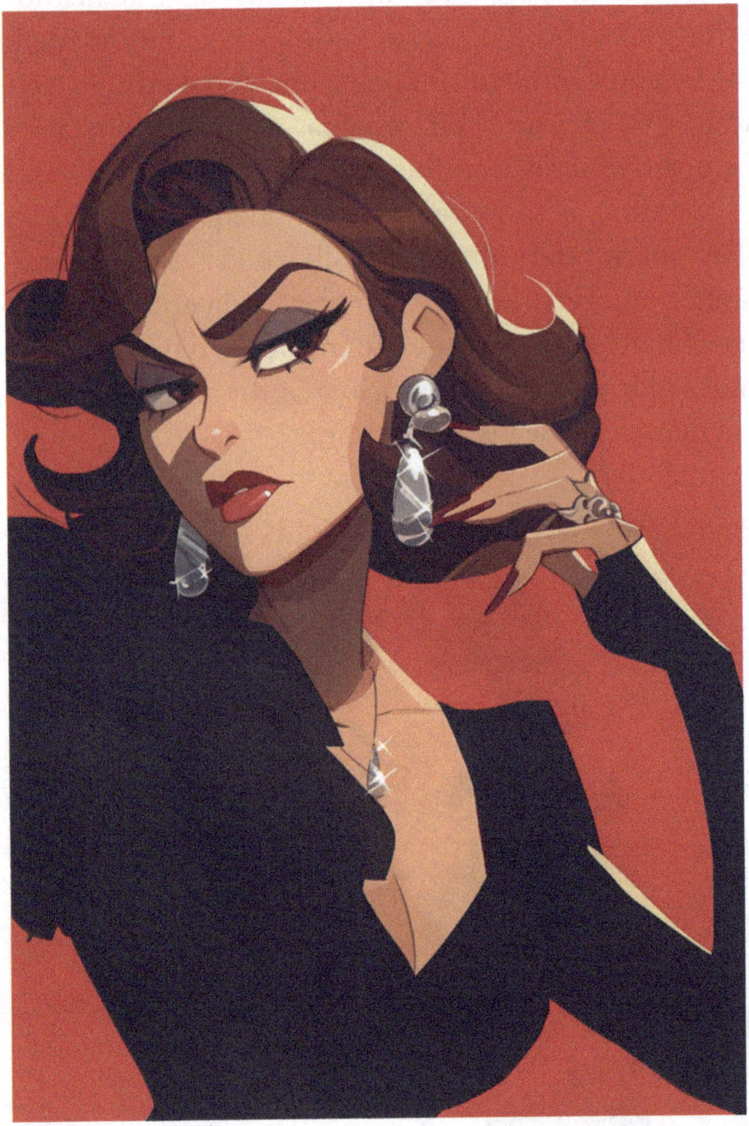

chapter 26

Reflections on what her story teaches us about resilience, transformation, and success

As we delve deeper into the inspiring journey of Joan Crawford, we uncover a wealth of wisdom and insights into the remarkable traits she possessed—resilience, transformation, and ultimate success. Her story serves as a testament to the power of determination, the capacity for personal growth, and the rewards that await those who embrace change and overcome adversity.

Joan's life was not defined by an easy path. From her challenging early years in Texas to her relentless pursuit of her dreams in Hollywood, she displayed an unwavering resilience that continues to inspire generations. Born into humble beginnings as Lucille Fay LeSueur, she faced financial hardships, an unstable family environment, and societal pressure. Yet, she never allowed these circumstances to dampen her spirit or derail her ambitions.

Facing a difficult childhood, Joan Crawford learned the importance of resilience early on. Her father abandoned the family, leaving her mother to provide for her and her two siblings. Poverty cast a long shadow over her early years, but she refused to let it define her. Instead, she saw it as an opportunity to transform her circumstances through hard work and determination.

In her teenage years, she found escape and hope at a dance school, which opened her eyes to the glimmering world of entertainment. Recognizing her love for performance, she set out to conquer Hollywood, relentlessly pursuing her dreams. However, the journey was not an easy one. Early in her career, she faced numerous rejections and setbacks, forcing her to confront her self-doubt and summon the inner strength to persevere.

Throughout her journey, Joan Crawford consistently demonstrated an extraordinary capacity for transformation. Her decision to adopt a new name was not merely a matter of convenience but a deliberate act of transformation. She shed her old identity, embracing the name Joan Crawford as a symbol of her reinvention. This transformation was not merely external, as she honed her craft, cultivated a strong sense of self, and evolved into a multifaceted artist.

Joan Crawford's career trajectory serves as a masterclass in adaptability and versatility. As Hollywood transitioned from silent films to talkies, many actors faltered, unable to transition smoothly into the new medium. But Crawford recognized the importance of evolving with the times. She leveraged her determination, sought voice lessons, and diligently practiced her craft to ensure her success in this new era. This willingness to embrace change and continuously reinvent herself set her apart from her peers.

Beyond her professional transformation, Joan's personal growth is equally inspiring. She recognized that success extended beyond external achievements; it required introspection and self-improvement. Embracing the power of education, she voraciously read books, attended art classes, and studied the craft of acting. This dedication to self-improvement was instrumental in shaping her into the exceptional actress she became and solidified her position as a respected figure within the entertainment industry.

However, Joan Crawford's path to success was not without its obstacles. In a highly competitive and ruthless industry, she faced professional setbacks and personal challenges. Critics scrutinized her every move, and rumors circulated about her personal life. Yet, even in the face of adversity, she demonstrated an unwavering resilience that propelled her forward. Rather than succumbing to defeat, she channeled her setbacks into motivation, striving to prove herself once again. Through sheer determination, she reclaimed her position in the limelight and delivered iconic performances that captured the hearts and minds of audiences worldwide.

The story of Joan Crawford teaches us invaluable lessons on resilience, transformation, and success. Firstly, it reminds us that resilience is not solely reserved for the fortunate few; rather, it can be nurtured and honed through perseverance, inner strength, and a refusal to let obstacles define our journey. Joan's ability to bounce back from setbacks and carry herself with grace and tenacity serves as a profound reminder of the heights that resilience can take us to.

Furthermore, her transformative journey illustrates the immense power of self-discovery and reinvention. Joan Crawford's story encourages us to embrace change, let go of past identities, and strive for personal growth. She exemplified the idea that it is never too late to redefine oneself, to shed preconceived notions, and to step into a new chapter of our lives where our true potential can be realized.

Lastly, Joan Crawford's tremendous success is a testament to the rewards that await those who combine relentless determination with unwavering passion. She was not an overnight sensation but achieved greatness through decades of hard work, sacrifice, and an unwavering belief in her own abilities. Her story inspires us to set audacious goals, to persevere in the face of adversity, and to trust in our own capacity to shape our destinies.

In conclusion, Joan Crawford's story serves as a profound reminder of the indomitable human spirit, our potential for transformation, and the level of success that can be attained through resilience and unwavering determination. Her journey continues to inspire countless individuals worldwide, encouraging them to embrace change, pursue their dreams with passion, and never lose sight of the incredible power that lies within themselves.

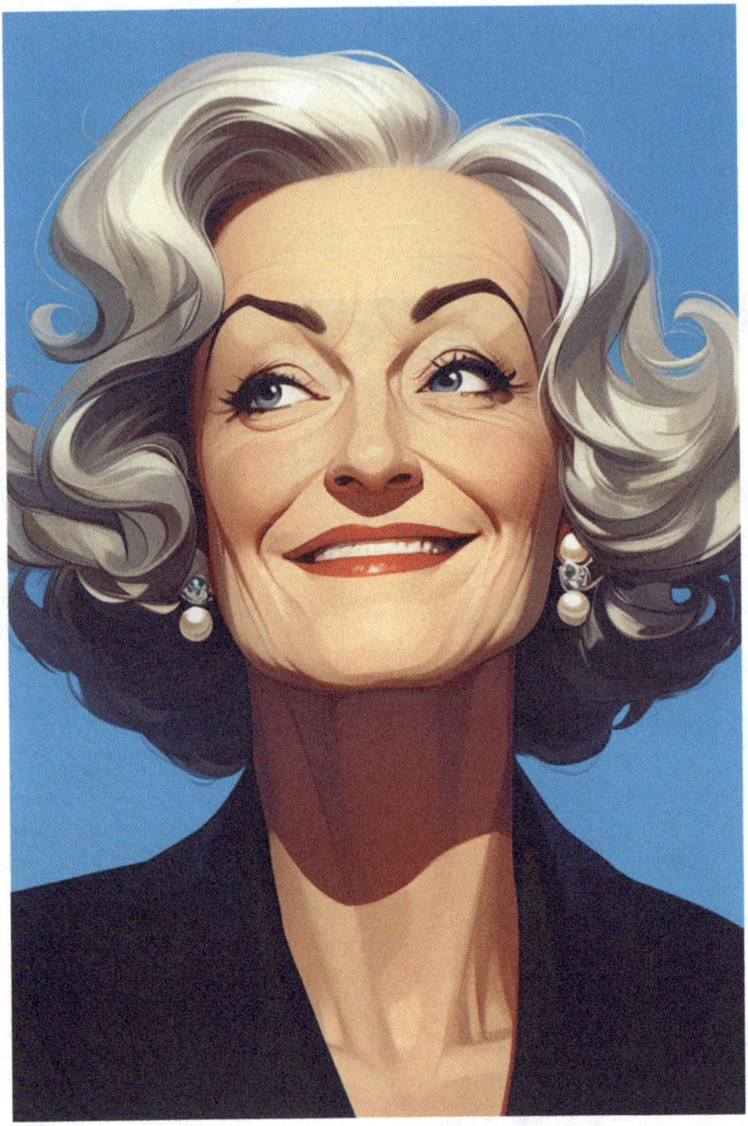

Made in the USA
Monee, IL
01 October 2024